Ten Plays +
Short, easy dramas for churches

Rosalie Sugrue

Philip Garside Publishing Ltd.

Copyright © 2013, 2018 & 2021 Rosalie Sugrue
Previously published as *Ten Plays*

All rights reserved.
Churches, preachers, worship and small group leaders
may freely copy and use the content in this book.

When doing so please credit:
Rosalie Sugrue — Ten Plays + (2021)

Rosalie appreciates knowing where her material is being used. Email her with your feedback:
sugrue.ro@gmail.com

If you want to include any of the material in this book
in a commercial or 'for profit' publication,
then please contact the publisher to arrange terms,
by emailing: books@pgpl.co.nz

International Print Edition
ISBN 978-1-98-857270-3

Updated and expanded 2021

Philip Garside Publishing Ltd
PO Box 17160
Wellington 6147
New Zealand

books@pgpl.co.nz www.pgpl.co.nz

Masks line drawings by:
Rosemary Garside

Kindle, ePub and PDF editions also available

Contents

Mary Jones' Walk 5
When The Treaty came to Mangungu 11
Easter Women 21
ANZAC Day 26
The Wesley Saga 32
How Lay Preaching Began 37
Go and Tell 43
A Peace Presentation 48
Mahlah and Sisters 61
Mahlah & Sisters (B) The Daughters of Zelophehad 67
Christmas Women 71
    Meditation 1 — Elizabeth (Mary's cousin) talks with Anna 71
    Meditation 2 — Anne (Mary's mother) 73
    Meditation 3 — Woman Traveller 75
    Meditation 4 — Inn-keeper's Wife 76
    Meditation 5 — Anna (the prophetess) 77
    Advent Service Outline 78
    Advent-Wreath Meditations 80
    An Advent Prayer (for two voices) 82
No Room 83
A Christmas Story 93
A Christmas Story (B) 100
    A Christmas Story (B) 1 – Man 100
    A Christmas Story (B) 2 – Woman 101
    A Christmas Story (B) 3 – Baby 102
    A Christmas Story (B) 4 – Inn-Keeper 103
    A Christmas Story (B) 5 – Bunch of Shepherds 104
    A Christmas Story (B) 6 – King 105
    A Christmas Story (B) 7 – Bunch of Wise-Guys 106
    A Christmas Story (B) 8 – Donkey 107
    A Christmas Story (B) 9 – Angel 108
Story Telling in Church 109
About these Plays 110
About the Author 112
    Also by Rosalie Sugrue from Philip Garside Publishing Ltd 113
Free PDF eBook edition offer 114

Ten Plays +

About the 2018 revised and expanded edition

Some of these plays have been revised to provide clearer instructions for staging them and to simplify or improve the dialogue.

ANZAC Day has been re-written.

A second version of *Mahlah & Sisters – The Daughters of Zelophehad* – has been added. It is the same story told in less words and is suitable for devotions at fellowships, house groups and youth groups.

A second version of *A Christmas Story* has also been provided, with 9 separate pages of 9 separate scripts for 9 people.

The typesetting of the book has also been updated. Māori words now have macrons where needed.

To help you stage these plays, the publisher is happy to provide a free PDF eBook edition of *Ten Plays* to anyone who has purchased a print copy. See the details of this offer at the end of the book.

New content in the 2021 edition

The new title **Ten Plays +** reflects that there are now 14 plays in this collection.

How Lay Preaching Began — A dialogue between John Wesley and his mother Susanna Wesley. John is upset that Thomas Maxwell, a layperson, has preached at The Foundery without his permission. It also includes notes about Susanna's later years, The Foundery and Lay Preachers.

Go and Tell — The Woman of Samaria meets other village women at the well and explains how her meeting with Jesus has changed her life. She also regains the friendship of these women who had previously shunned her.

Story Telling in Church gives readers suggestions for easy and simple ways to add drama to Bible stories in church.

Mary Jones' Walk

Suitable for Youth and Children, Bible Sunday, Church Parade, or Family Service

Cast: Narrator, Mary Jones, Mrs Jones, seven wayfarers (A-G), Rev Charles, Mrs Charles. (12 people)

• • •

Mary begins at the front left of the church and walks down the aisles encountering people along the way. She loops back to the front right for Bala.

Narrator: The year is 1800. The place is a tiny village in North Wales. Most of the people are poor and know very little about the world. They only speak the Welsh language, but we have translated it for you.

Mrs Jones: I'm so proud of you Mary. *(Hug)*

Mary: Goodbye Mother.

Mrs Jones: God be with you Mary. *(Wave)*

A: You're up early Mary. Where are you going?

Mary: I'm going to Bala.

A: Bala! That's 25 miles away. It will take you all day to walk to Bala.

Mary: That's why I'm staring so early.

B: Hullo Mary. Why are you wearing your shoes round your neck?

Mary: I'm walking twenty-five miles. I don't want my shoes to wear out before I get there. I'm keeping these shoes for the streets of Bala.

B: God bless you Mary.

C: Hullo Mary. Are you going a-visiting?

Mary: Yes, I'm going to visit the Reverend Thomas Charles. He lives in Bala.

C: That's a long way to go.

Mary: I know but I'm used to walking.

C: Good luck Mary.

D: Good morning young lady. And what might you be doing?

Mary: I'm going Bala to buy a Bible.

D: Can you read? There's not much learning round here.

Mary: When I was eight, a school opened in the village next to mine. It took me an hour to walk there, and an hour back, but I learnt to read.

D: Well, good luck to you young lady.

E: Good afternoon girl. Where are you going and what are you doing?

Mary: I've learnt how to read and I'm going to Bala to buy a Bible.

E: The Bible is full of hard words. It's not like reading from the blackboard at school. Reading a Bible is right difficult.

Mary: I know it's difficult, but I've been practising. I've been practising for years. My neighbour, Mrs Evans, has a Bible. She lets me read it in her house on Sunday afternoons.

E: You are a lucky girl to have such a good neighbour.

Mary: Indeed, I am very lucky. Mrs Evens is very kind.

E: May good fortune stay with you.

Mary: Thank-you Mam.

F: Good afternoon lassie. What is your business, may I ask?

Mary: I'm going to Bala to buy a Bible.

F: A Bible! But a Bible is very expensive.

Mary: I know. I have been saving for years.

F: How could you earn money?

Mary: When I was little, I ran errands for people, and I told them I was saving up for a Bible. I did weeding and knitting and child-minding. Then a kind neighbour gave me some hens. I've been selling eggs and raising chickens for six years and now I have enough money to buy a Bible.

F: That's a fine effort to be sure. God bless you lassie.

Mary: Thank-you Mam.

G: Good evening traveller. Can I help you?

Mary: Is this the town of Bala? I'm looking for the Reverend Thomas Charles.

G: Yes, this is Bala. Turn down the next street, go over the hill and you will see the church spire. The Reverend lives next to the church.

Mary: Thank-you Sir. *(Put on shoes, walk, and knock)*

Others move to front right using side aisles if possible.

Mary: Good evening Mam. May I speak to the Reverend, please?

Mrs Charles: It's getting late. Is the matter urgent?

Mary: Yes Mam, it is urgent. I've walked from Llan-fi-han-gely Pennant to see him.

Mrs Charles: You'd better come inside then. Thomas, there is a girl to see you.

Rev Charles: What do you want child?

Mary: Please Sir, I want to buy a Bible.

Rev Charles: I'm sorry child but I don't have any Bibles left.

Mary: No Bibles left but…it can't be… *(Cry)*

Mrs Charles: She's walked all the way from Llan-fi-han-gely Pennant.

Rev Charles: That's a good twenty-five miles. No wonder the girl is in such a state.

Mrs Charles: There, there child, don't cry. I'll get you a nice cup of tea.

Mary: Thank-you, but I came to Bala to buy a Bible.

Mrs Charles: You have a cuppa and tell the Reverend all about it. *(Exit)*

Rev Charles: Sit here girl and tell us about yourself.

Mary: My name is Mary Jones. I'm fifteen years old. *(Dry eyes)*

Rev Charles: And who is your father Mary?

Mary: My father was a weaver, but he died when I was four. I live with my mother.

Rev Charles: Do you go to church regularly Mary? *(Mrs Charles gives Mary a cup)*

Mary: Oh yes Sir. Mother and I go to Chapel every Sunday. That's how I got to love the Bible. I wanted to learn to read so I could read the Bible myself. Our Pastor made the arrangements for me to go to school in Tyn-Ddol. I've worked very hard and I do so want a Bible.

Rev Charles: I do have one Bible left but it has been promised to someone else. Dear child you must understand that Bibles in Welsh are very hard to come by. But you can't leave now. It will be dark before you get home. You must stay here for the night. Mrs Charles will find you a place to sleep.

Mrs Charles takes Mary off right; Rev Charles lies down; the Wayfarers having quietly come to the front by a side aisle, if possible, form a line.

Mary Jones' Walk

Narrator: That night the Reverend Thomas Charles had a vivid dream.

Wayfarers speak into microphone and file past the sleeping Rev shaking their heads.

Mrs Jones: God be with you Mary.

A: Bala is twenty-five miles from Llan-fi-han-gely Pennant.

B: She walked barefoot.

C: She walked all day.

D: She learnt to read so she could read the Bible – two hours of walking to get to school.

E: She practiced Bible reading every Sunday afternoon.

F: She saved for six years – running errands, knitting, raising hens, selling eggs.

G: She walked barefoot so her shoes would be respectable for you.

Mrs Charles: You can't let that girl go home without a Bible.

All: She came to Bala to buy a Bible. She came to Bala to buy a Bible… *(Chanting)*

Rev wakes up, rummages round and finds a Bible.

Narrator: Reverend Thomas Charles gave Mary Jones his last Bible. But he did more than that.

Mary goes off clutching Bible

Rev Charles: I told Mary's story to a Religious Society in London. I explained how difficult it is to get Bibles in the Welsh language. The men agreed to help make Bibles more available for Welsh speaking people.

Then, another minister, Reverend Joseph Hughes, jumped up and said, 'If Wales, why not the world! Let's make Bibles

Ten Plays +

available to all people who want to read God's word in their own language.'

Narrator: So, in March 1804 the British and Foreign Bible Society was formed.

Ever since people have given money to support the distribution of Bibles in many languages. Our Holy Bible has been translated into more languages than any other book, thanks in part to the determination of one young girl.

Mary comes back holding her Bible.

All: The Bible is the world's most read book. Thank you, Mary Jones.

• • •

Production suggestions

- Mary wears an apron and Welsh hat made from black paper; brim lined with white crepe-paper ruff. Shoes with laces knotted together hang round her neck. She wears or carries a microphone.

- Wayfarers spaced round the church aisles read their words (loudly) from a small card.

When The Treaty came to Mangungu

A story based around historical facts.

A play for four female voices and one male, plus reader.

Characters: Reader, Manu, Emma, Mother, Mrs White, Rev John Hobbs

• • •

Reader: In 1839 the Wesleyan Mission station at Mangungu comprised a clutch of modest buildings, gardens, orchard, cows, pigs, goats and hens. The mission had its own printing press, brick-kiln and saw pits. The pride of the missionaries was a wooden church that could hold eight hundred people. The joy of the mission women was the new Georgian styled homestead that stood tall on a hill overlooking the Hokianga harbour. Two girls are sitting on the lawn.

Manu: The walls of your house are so white I can hardly look at them. You're lucky to live in that big house. The coloured glass round the front door is so pretty, and the upstairs windows look like two eyes peeping out of the roof.

Emma: My father was a carpenter before he became a Minister. I guess we are lucky that our old house caught on fire when the Turner's house burnt down. Father told the Missionary Society that our mission needed a house good enough for important visitors. But a big house means lots of work. You are lucky Manu because you don't have to clean windows, scrub floors, wash dishes or polish furniture. You're as free as a bird!

Reader: They both laughed because *manu* is Māori for bird.

Emma was the eldest child in the Hobbs family. Now, she had to help with the young ones more than ever, because her mother had just had another baby boy. Emma hoped the new baby would fill the gap left by the one that died last year, that had made her mother sad and ill. Counting baby Edward there were six children in the Hobbs family. Richard was seven and Phebe four. Her other sisters, Margaretta eight, and Marianne nine, did everything together, and didn't have Emma's responsibilities.

Emma and Manu had met at the mission school. Manu was eleven, the eldest child in her family and the same age as Emma. Both were quick learners. Emma knew lots of Māori words and Manu picked up English as if she had been born speaking it. Whenever they could the two friends went exploring together. However, Emma didn't have much free time and when she did it usually ended like this.

Mother: Emma, you have got your skirt wet again. And just look at your boots, they're covered in mud! I wish you wouldn't play such messy games. Go and get cleaned up.

Emma: Yes Mother. I'm sorry Mother…if only I didn't have to wear long dresses. Can't I go without my boots, please?

Mother: Certainly not.

Emma: Manu has never worn shoes in her whole life.

Mother: Ours ways are different.

Emma: Manu doesn't live with her parents. She lives in a tiny hut with her Grandmother. Her parents said she was a gift for her grandmother. She still has loads of time to swing on vines in the bush and watch the fish darting between the mangroves. Manu's grandmother knows stories about taniwha and fairy-folk. I haven't even met my grandparents.

Mother: I know dear, but never forget you do have grandparents, and uncles and aunts and cousins. I miss them very much. England is a very long way away, but they know about us and pray for us just as we pray for them. The best we can do is to remember them by our customs. You know what your father says.

Emma: 'I expect my children to be an example at all times.'

When The Treaty came to Mangungu

Reader: Rev John Hobbs was a stern man of high principles. He was compassionate and fair in his dealings with Māori and took time to understand the Māori ways. As a linguist he was superb and had mastered the manner of Māori oratory. He was also a fine musician, and skilled in building and horticulture. Like all ministers of his time, he preached sermons warning people against the dangers of sin, but his passion was the good news.

Hobbs: For there is neither Jew or Greek, bond or free, there is neither male nor female: for ye are all one in Christ' (Galatians 3:28.) This passage tells us all people should be friends, no matter what their race, colour or status. Being one in Christ does not mean all people should be the same, it means we must help one another, learn from the other, and care for each other.

Reader: John Hobbs firmly believed what he preached but had trouble practising it with one of his fellow missionaries, William White. White continually challenged Hobbs' position as head missioner. White had an interest in commerce and was intemperate in many ways. However, White's wife, Eliza, William's junior by seventeen years, was loved by everyone. She started the class for girls at the mission. The children called her Māta Waiti. She taught the four Rs – Reading, 'Riting, 'Rithmetic and Religion, but her favourite lesson was sewing. Māta Waiti was very particular about sewing.

Mrs White: Sewing is one of the most important skills a girl can have. One day you will be making your own clothes, and taking care of the mending, but first you must learn the stitches.

Reader: Sewing made more sense than chanting tables or practising handwriting on small slates with squeaky slate-pencils. The girls worked hard and soon mastered the basic stitches.

Mrs White: A shipment of fabric arrived a few days ago. I have a calico square for each of you. Now you can make your own wall sampler, something you can keep and be proud of.

Manu: What is a wall sampler?

Mrs White: A sampler is a sample of different stitches. A wall sampler is a sewing-picture with a message that can be framed and hung on a wall. I want everyone to choose a favourite text from the Bible. Then you must copy it very carefully onto your piece of calico.

Manu: Let's choose the same text. What is your favourite one Emma?

Emma: I think my favourite is 'Ye are all one in Christ.'

Reader: The girls stitched the words in blue thread. Manu bordered hers with berries made from tiny red knots while Emma worked yellow flowers in lazy-daisy stitch. It took a long time because although everyone liked sewing other lessons were considered more important.

One summer day Māti Waiti wrote Monday, 10th February 1840, on the blackboard. The girls had begun to copy *The quick brown fox jumps over the lazy dog* when Emma's mother rushed into the schoolroom and spoke excitedly to Mrs White.

Mrs White: Stop work children. Remember last week, I told you that a great white chief from England had arrived at Waitangi to talk with the Māori chiefs, and he wanted to meet with some of the Hokianga chiefs. Well, something very important has happened. You tell them Mrs Hobbs.

Mother: The Māori and Pākehā chiefs who met at Waitangi have agreed to live in harmony, obeying the laws of Queen Victoria. Most of the Māori chiefs signed a parchment called The Treaty of Waitangi. The paper is going to be taken round the whole country so all chiefs can add their marks. Mr Hobson, the great white chief, is going to bring the Treaty here. Mangungu has been chosen as the next big meeting place. It is a great honour. Mr Hobson and his officials arrived at Waimate on horseback yesterday. They will be here tomorrow afternoon.

Mrs White: There is much to do, and you can help. School will be closed until the visitors have gone.

When The Treaty came to Mangungu

Reader: The Mission Station buzzed with busyness. The children picked all the ripe fruit in the orchard. Bread was baked and meat was roasted. The two straw beehives were raided. Mangungu had the first honeybees in New Zealand. Fresh honey would be a real treat for the Governor's party. The big house was scrubbed and polished from top to bottom. Straw mattresses were stacked in readiness to turn the parlour into a dormitory for the guests.

The Governor arrived by boat around 4pm Tuesday amid a flotilla of craft carrying missionaries, chiefs, and principal settlers who had met the official party at Waihou. Twenty people took dinner in the Mission House dining-room that evening. Miss Mary Ann Bumby, sister of the General-Superintendent of the Wesleyan Mission in New Zealand, was the hostess. The Rev John Bumby was in Australia on Church business.

Crowds of people camped in the mission grounds. This was an established practise as every Saturday night two or three hundred Māori gathered in readiness for the Sunday church services, but this crowd was not to be measured in hundreds.

Emma: There must be a hundred million people out there.

Hobbs: There are not that many people in the world Emma. But it is an amazing sight. The staff have made an estimate of around two and a half thousand, and over 400 chiefs.

Emma: It looks like all the people in the whole of New Zealand are meeting at our place.

Reader: Chiefs arrived in cloaks of feathers or dog-skin. Others wore bright blankets. Important Māori women came with feathers in their hair. Pākehā men wore suits and tall hats and the Pākehā ladies wore their Sunday gowns and bonnets.

At nine o'clock, on Wednesday 12th of February, a table and chairs were placed on the Mission House veranda. The most important chiefs were invited to come and sit on the mission lawn. Then the speeches began. Reverend Hobbs was the translator. Emma felt proud that her father had such an important job. Dignified English gentlemen spoke about mighty Queen Victoria who lived in a magnificent meeting house far across the sea. She had great mana and would keep law and order and protect the people. Visiting missionaries, wearing black robes, talked about truth and justice. Māori chiefs delivered long orations, some thumped taiaha as they told of ancestors and their connection with the land. Some speakers shouted and sounded angry; others sounded sad.

Manu: These speeches are never going to stop, let's go and look at the boats in the harbour.

Emma: I've never seen so many boats, or so many different kinds of boats.

Manu: Rowboats, sailboats, rafts, great waka and small canoes.

Emma: The boats are as well dressed as the people. The flags make splendid decorations.

Reader: The sun was sinking, and the sky flamed red and gold as the friends wandered up through the brown grass to the bush-topped hill.

Emma: Listen, the speeches have stopped. Let's see what is happening.

Manu: How can we get to the front of all these people?

Emma: Follow me. We can go round the crowd and get in the back door. If we peep through the coloured glass beside the front door we won't be seen.

Manu: The chiefs are writing on the paper, lots and lots of chiefs.

Reader: That night Emma couldn't sleep. The children were on the hard floor of their parents' room. The younger girls had fallen asleep, but the noise of the crowd kept Emma's awake. Every hour she counted the chimes of the parlour clock. It was after the last stoke of twelve when her father slipped into bed beside her mother.

Hobbs: Oh Jane, I hope we have done the right thing. They trust me. I tried to prepare our chiefs for this eventuality. In the past week I've spent hours with Nene explaining the advantages of British sovereignty. Late today other chiefs asked my advice and I said it would be good for Māori. It was then that they started to sign, seventy of them. Forty-three chiefs signed at Waitangi. This treaty gives Europeans the right to live here and protects the indigenous rights of the Māori, but can everyone be trusted to honour the treaty? Did I do the right thing?

Reader: Emma kept as still as a mouse, anxious to hear her mother's reply.

Mother: Of course you did the right thing John. It's what we have been praying for. We are now one people. He iwi tahi tātou. Mr Hobson's words when he shook hands with the chiefs. We will just have to work at it to make it come true.'

Reader: There was a silence and Emma knew her parents were holding each other tight.

The next day was even more exciting.

Mother: We are all going on a picnic today. We're going up the river to Hokere.

Emma: Can Manu come with us?

Hobbs: If she comes here before we leave, she may, but you must help your mother now.

Reader: Emma kept her fingers crossed as best she could while helping dress the little ones. Manu appeared in time. They all packed into the mission boat with the other mission families and sailed upstream. What a picnic it was! The official count was three thousand including men, women and children. Proceedings began with a great haka. The hills echoed to the sound of fifteen hundred warriors. The officials stood up in their boat and called for three cheers.

Hobbs: Hip-hip

Everyone: Hooray! *[x 3]*

Hobbs: Gentlemen, please remove your hats for a prayer of thanksgiving. Gracious God, for all the mercies Thou hast given us, for the joy that comes from peace and the bounty of this feast may we be truly grateful. Bless this food to our use and us to Thy service. Amen.

Reader: The hāngī pits were opened and the feast began.

Manu: This is like the feeding of the five thousand in the Bible.

Emma: Only better, because we've got more than just loaves and fishes to eat.

Reader: Warriors and officials issued portions of pork, potatoes and rice, followed by sugar treats. After the eating came races and games. Emma and Manu won the girls' three-legged race. Late in the day volley of guns was fired to remind everyone that this was a time of great rejoicing. From across the harbour at Kohukohu, came a reply volley.

Emma: The sound is solemn and happy at the same time.

Manu: It's like singing Āmine, Āmine, Āmine, at the end of a service.

Emma: I think this has been the best day of my life.

Manu: Me too.

Reader: That night the Hobbs girls were back in their own room. Before blowing out the candle, Emma gazed at her sampler hanging over the bed she shared with her sisters.

Emma: All one in Christ – one people, all different, and all friends.

• • •

When The Treaty came to Mangungu

Notes

Mangungu is pronounced: Mar-noo-noo. The Mission ceased in 1855. A small wooden church remains on the site.

The fully restored Mission House belongs to the New Zealand Historic Places Trust and is open to the public on holiday afternoons.

The grand picnic at Hokere really happened. Although Rev John Hobbs designed and oversaw the building of the Mission House his family did not occupy it until January 1841. Apart from 'Manu' all the people named in this story were real people. The gathering at Mangungu was the largest of all the 'Te Tiriti' meetings. More chiefs signed The Treaty on the 12th of February than any other day. By the 4th of March the original parchment was full. Eight further copies of the Treaty were taken to different parts of New Zealand by Officials or Missionaries. It took nine months to gather about five hundred signatures.

The Treaty of Waitangi: Article 4

A fourth article was added to the Māori text of the Treaty signed at Waitangi, at the request of Bishop Jean Baptiste Pompallier. In Māori the fourth article said:

> "E mea ana te Kāwana ko ngā whakapono katoa o Ingarani, o ngā Wēteriana, o Rōma, me te ritenga Māori hoki e tiakina ngatahitia e ia"

which means

> "The Governor says that the several faiths (beliefs) of England, of the Wesleyans, of Rome and also of Māori custom shall alike be protected by him."

This article guaranteed religious freedom for all in the new nation, including Māori.

Ten Plays +

References

- *The Treaty of Waitangi*, T. L. Buick, 1936
- *John Hobbs 1800-1883*, T. M. I. Williment, 1985
- *The Treaty of Waitangi,* Claudia Orange, 1987
- *Methodism and the Treaty,* Barry E Jones, 1989
- *Return to Mangungu,* Wesley Historical Society, 1990
- *Christianity in Aotearoa,* Allan K Davidson, 1991
- *Aotearoa New Zealand: Defining Moments in the Gospel-Culture encounter*, Allan K Davidson, 1996
- *The Treaty of Waitangi* – Information Programme, State Services Commission, 2006

Production suggestions

- Costumes are not necessary
- May be performed by children or adults, ideally both (including a local presbyter)
- Narrator sits centre wearing clip-on microphone – extra children at feet as if listening to a story. (These children join in the cheering and may make other appropriate noises.)
- Emma & Manu at pulpit microphone; adults round lectern microphone

Easter Women

A play reading for Lent, that feels into possible thoughts of the women who witnessed the Crucifixion.

Requires a Narrator and five adult female readers: Joanna, Mary of Nazareth, Salome, Mary Magdalene and the Other Mary.

Once there was
an embryonic time when the
Christian faith was an unborn reality
& ordinary people lived hard lives
in trimesters of quiet desperation
but the seed of hope matured &
some men followed hope's call
& some women nurtured hope
The birth pains of Christianity
were worse than anything
imagined by the faithful
Yet the women did
what women do
Supported the
one in labour
regardless
of outcome.

• • •

Narrator: *(Introduction)* Who were 'the women' of that first Easter? The Bible is ambiguous as to exactly who witnessed the crucifixion and attended the tomb. Each Gospel gives a different list, but one thing we are sure of is, women followers were present. No lists of male disciples are recorded. The men, so prominent at the last supper, almost disappear when the chips are down.

The women who followed Jesus were independent women, independent of spirit and independent of means. We don't know how many there were, but records of the early church assure us women were among its leaders. Luke tells us early in his Gospel that 'women provided for Jesus and the disciples out of their means.'

In the Easter narratives each Gospel names three or four women. Only Mary Magdalene is named in all four accounts. Three to five Marys are mentioned, but strangely Mary of Bethany is not among them. Scholars differ as to who Mary Magdalene was. There are theories – she was a prostitute; she had a mental illness and was cured by Jesus; she was from a town called Magdala; she was Mary Magna – the Great Mary thus named to distinguish her from lesser Marys. Some say the 'great' Mary is another name for the Mary who was sister to Martha and Lazarus. What could make any Mary greater than Mary the mother of Jesus? Regardless of your conclusion, the one the Easter narratives call 'Mary Magdalene' had a very special relationship with Jesus.

John tells us the mother of Jesus was present along with her sister. Matthew mentions 'the mother of Zebedee's children.' Mark gives us the name Salome.

Mark and Matthew mention a Mary who is the mother of James and Joseph and John mentions a Mary who is the wife of Clopas. At the tomb Matthew refers to a woman he calls 'the other Mary.' Luke also names a Joanna, previously identified as the wife of Chuza from the court of Herod.

With all these women held in tension I invite you to flex your imaginations and listen in on five women who may have shared a room on that Saturday night so long ago. Our group comprises: Mary of Nazareth – the mother of Jesus, Mary Magdalene alias Mary of Bethany, the 'other' Mary, Joanna and Salome.

The Sabbath ended at sundown. To be in Jerusalem for Passover should have been a pinnacle of religious celebration. To these women no Sabbath had ever been sadder. Joanna expresses what they've all been thinking.

Joanna: Why, why did he come to Jerusalem?

Mary of Nazareth: I tried to stop him, I tried, but would he listen to his mother!

Salome: Always the stubborn one.

Mary Magdalene: He knew it would end this way – he was prepared, and so was I. Didn't you realise when I anointed his head? I was trying to tell those men Jesus is a king. He said his kingdom was not of this world. They didn't get it!

Salome: Why did you anoint his feet?

Mary of Magdalene: That was personal. My place was at his feet listening, imploring, loving. I can't bear to think of those feet…

Other Mary: You cry Mary. If you need to cry, it is the best thing to do. But take comfort in knowing his feet will never know pain again. Joanna provided the very best oils and spices and we wrapped him with great care. It was the finest tomb I've ever seen.

Mary Magdalene: Yes, yes, I'm so grateful to you both, and to Joseph of Arimathea. I was just so distraught when I saw his battered body up close. I couldn't do what had to be done. I know you spared no expense Joanna. His burial was fit for a king.

Joanna: It was my privilege, Mary. It was the least I could do. I am deeply honoured that I have had the means to help support the community these past two years.

Salome: How have you been able to provide for us? You never speak of your former life other than to say you have your husband's blessing. Who is your husband? Will you tell us now?

Joanna: My husband is Chuza an official in the court of Herod. One day a prisoner came under his care. They said the prisoner was a mad man, but my husband saw it wasn't so. The man was a preacher, a prophet and skilled in the ways of understanding.

Chuza enjoys a good debate and he became impressed by the man's perceptions.

Other Mary: Who was the prisoner?

Joanna: They called him John the Baptist. We both witnessed the terrible manipulations of Herodias. I vowed to do something to get back at her. When I heard that the one of whom the Baptist had spoken was preaching nearby, I went to hear what he had to say. As I listened, I realised revenge is less worthy than trying to make amends. I told Chuza I wanted to become a follower. Chuza thought it over carefully and said, go if this is your wish. This court is not a safe place for anyone especially a young woman. Go and I will help you support the cousin of my ill-treated prisoner.

Other Mary: It is truly amazing the effect Jesus has on people. Here you are a woman from the royal court and me a fisherman's wife, and both of us moved to follow Jesus. Class meant nothing to him, and now nothing to us. I never dreamed my Clopas would encourage me to leave home, but he saw something special in Jesus. Clopas was proud that Jesus invited our James to be one of the chosen twelve. I was flabbergasted. The boy was expected to go into the family business. But Clopas said he and Jose could manage on their own, and as James was so young, I'd better go to keep an eye on him. I want to know more of this Jesus he said. Once a young man leaves home there is no holding him, but you will return with amazing stories…how can I return with this story?

Salome: By remembering how life-changing Jesus was. Amazing is the word for Jesus. Never forget the wonders we have seen and how Jesus affects people. You know what a stormy fellow my Zebedee is, always ranting and raving, yet he treated Jesus quite differently. Even as a child there was something about Jesus that calmed my Zeb. Remember, dear sister that time Jesus got lost. It was the time we took the boys to Jerusalem for the Passover. Zebedee fair blew his top at James and John for not telling us where their cousin was. The boys should have said he wasn't with them, but boys will be boys. I feared Zebedee would really get stuck into Jesus, but no, he was too interested in what the child had been up to. My Zeb recognized Jesus was a child of superior ability. He always was an ambitious man. Had such ambitions for his own sons. I guess it rubbed off on me. They were cousins but how I regret asking Jesus to give our sons a place of privilege. I just didn't understand. I was so wrong!

Mary of Nazareth: Hush, Salome, you have always been the outspoken one, but you are a dear sister, a good wife and a fine mother. Jesus loves his Aunty Salome, even though he has refused to call you aunt for years. It's just his way. He is sharp at times, but his love runs deep. You know how he cares for me and my girls, yet he refused to acknowledge us when we asked to see him. Who are my mother, sisters and brothers he asked? I was so hurt, but later I understood. It was his way of saying we are not to be identified by whom we are related to. Everyone is a person in their own right. Each of us has value in the sight of God. We here are all strong individuals. The men were unable to face the full horror of the past two days, but we have been given the strength to cope. We are a community, a sisterhood of strong women. We will remember his words. We will cherish them in our hearts. He will live on in our actions. I won't have the life of my precious child wasted. And now we must sleep for who knows what awaits us in the morning.

Mary Magdalene: I would so like to hold him again.

• • •

Production Suggestions
- Narrator at pulpit microphone.
- Others grouped round another microphone, sitting or standing.
- Costume: long scarves draped over heads.

ANZAC Day

A play reading that reflects on war

Four characters: Mum, Dad, son Jamie, daughter Amber.

• • •

Jamie is sitting at the table engrossed with an electronic device; Mum stands behind the table, she wears an apron and holds a cloth (or another kitchen item) and looks busy.

Amber enters wearing a uniform, or a symbol of uniform (hat scarf etc), she removes her back-pack with a thud.

Jamie: Why are you wearing your Girl Guide *(or Girl's Brigade)* uniform?

Amber: I've been selling red poppies in the mall. Our company was asked to help.

Sits at the other end of the table, chair turned towards congregation.

Jamie: Yay! It's ANZAC day tomorrow, no school, we get a holiday.

Mum: We will be going to the Citizens Service at the War Memorial in the morning.

Amber: I am going to be carrying the Girl Guide flag in the parade.

Mum: That is an honour! We will be proud of you.

Jamie: I like marching in the parade with the band, but the speeches get really boring, they go on and on.

Mum: Those speeches are important; you should try listening. If we don't know our history, we are in danger of repeating it.

Jamie: I know what ANZAC is about – soldiers who died years ago. We learn that stuff at school. Hundreds of New Zealand and Australian soldiers died at Gallipoli, it's a place in Turkey, and it was ages ago.

ANZAC Day

Amber: It was exactly one hundred and ____ years ago. [25 April 1915]

Jamie: You are such a know all. History is full of old wars but there aren't wars now – not fighting wars that New Zealander soldiers are in.

Amber: There are!

Jamie: Are not!

Amber: Are so!

Jamie: Are not!

Amber: Are so!

Mum: Stop it you two. I won't have a war in my kitchen! But the sad fact is there has never been a time when there hasn't been a war somewhere in the world. New Zealand soldiers are fighting at this very moment.

Jamie: Are they being killed?

Mum: In recent times there haven't been large numbers of Kiwis killed overseas. But there have been some and ANZAC Day remembers them too.

Amber: If there have always been wars why is the ANZAC war called the First World War?

Mum: That war was not just about the ANZACs. It involved soldiers and citizens from many countries. It was called The Great War and was expected to end all wars, but a generation later, with new technology The Second World War made an even bigger impact on the whole world.

Jamie: I don't know why we make such a fuss about the First World War. It didn't happen here, and it's got nothing to do with us.

Dad: *(Arriving home from work)* Hullo everyone, what has nothing to do with us.

Jamie & Amber: Hi Dad.

Mum: Hullo James. Jamie thinks the First World War has nothing to do with us?

Dad puts down his briefcase and sits behind the table.

Dad: Does he indeed! Well, perhaps young James needs a little history lesson. Why, my son, were you Christened James George?

Jamie: Because James is your name.

Dad: Correct, and James is also the name of my father and his father. It's a family tradition. Your great-grandfather was known as Jim and he fought in the Second World War. Jim was captured and spent two terrible years in a prisoner of war camp in Italy. His father, your great-great grandfather was also named James, but he got called Jimmy, and he fought in the First World War.

Jamie: Were they all Christened James George?

Dad: No, they all had different middle names. But your middle name does have a story. The James who was known as Jimmy had a younger brother called George. And young George also went to the First World War, but George never came back. He was killed at the Battle of the Somme in France.

Mum: We should show the children George's name on the War Memorial.

Amber: Can we see it tomorrow?

Dad: No, it's not on our local memorial it is on the memorial in my home town. I will show you when we visit your Grandparents in the school holidays.

Amber: Are there a lot of war memorials in New Zealand?

Mum: Almost every town in New Zealand has a war memorial. When World War 1 broke out young men from every town were encouraged to join the armed forces. New Zealand ended up sending more soldiers to that war than any other county on a proportional basis.

Dad: Every Kiwi family that has been here for more than three generations is likely to have a relation on a war memorial somewhere in New Zealand.

Jamie: It would have been exciting going to war.

Dad: That is what a lot of young men thought but they soon changed their minds. Ordinary soldiers spent much of their time digging ditches, called trenches, to give protection from the enemy guns. They had to sleep in wet clothes. Rats kept trying to get at their food. Soldiers could be shot for disobeying orders, or even for appearing frightened.

Mum: In my opinion the only way to stop wars is for everyone to refuse to fight.

Jamie: But the bad guys wouldn't stop being bad. With no one to stop them the baddies would win!

Mum: Most people don't want to be bad. When people agree to fight, they are forced to do bad things. That is why being a soldier is not an easy choice. Some questions don't have right answers. People just have to do what they believe is the best thing to do.

Amber: If there is no right answer it must be hard to work out what is the best thing to do.

Mum: Very hard. My great-grandfather went to the First World war, but my grandfather and his brother refused to fight. They knew that their father had to kill and how he hated it. Killing people can't be right, they said, our consciences tell us it's wrong. Men who said that were called conscientious objectors, or 'conchies.' People said they were cowards, and they were put in prison for refusing to go to war. Some were fed bread and water and nothing else. You had to be brave to be a Conchie.

Amber: It all sounds horrible. I'm glad women didn't have to go to war.

Dad: Ah, but some women did volunteer – not as fighters, they went as nurses to care for the wounded, but of some of them got killed along with ordinary people who lived in the countries where the fighting was. It's not just soldiers who are killed.

Mum: And it is important that you know about it.

Amber: That's what our teacher said. We have to do ANZAC projects – make a book with illustrations. It has to be finished by the end of the holidays. I don't know what I'm going to do.

Mum: Learning some facts might help. You have 10 minutes before dinner.

Dad: Good idea! I will pay $1 for each statistic you find for World War 1, and Amber, yours have to be different from Jamie's.

During a suitable pause of 1-3 minutes,
Amber gets out her phone and both children do vigorous tapping and
scrolling while WW1 marching music is played and
(if practical) WW1 photos are shown on PowerPoint.

Dad: OK, time's up. What have you found out?

Children deliver facts in a competitive sounding way

Jamie: The war began in June 1914 and lasted until November 1918.

Amber: In 1914 the total population of New Zealand was just over one million.

Jamie: 120,000 New Zealanders enlisted in the Armed Force

Amber: 103,000 Kiwis served overseas.

Jamie: 18,500 New Zealanders died in the war.

Amber: More than 2,700 died at Gallipoli.

Jamie: 12,500 died on the Western Front. That's where great-great-great Uncle George was killed.

Amber: 550 nurses served with the New Zealand Forces.

ANZAC Day

Jamie: 41,000 new Zealanders were wounded.

Amber: There are about 500 civic war memorials in New Zealand.

Jamie: That's all I've got.

Amber: I could have found more but there wasn't time.

Dad: And just as well or I would be broke. *(Takes out wallet)*

Mum: Great work kids.

Amber: I've got a project idea! When we go on holiday, I'm going to take photos of War Memorials and make a War Memorial scrapbook.

Jamie: I'm named after a war hero. I'm going to find out more about my truly great Uncle.

Dad: Granddad will be able to tell you some family stories, but you could start by looking at our family tree on-line. It's now possible to access personal war records from genealogy sites.

Mum: I have already started researching my family's Conscientious Objectors. I intend writing their story. All brave stories need to be heard.

Amber: If we don't know our history, we are in danger of repeating it!

• • •

Additional ending

Cast stands and is joined by the Worship Leader who reads the 1st verse of *Hymn for ANZAC Day*, Jamie reads 2nd verse, Mum 3rd verse, Dad 4th verse, Amber 5th verse.

Suggested Hymn:

- *Honour the Dead: Hymn for ANZAC Day*. Music: © Colin Gibson 2005 Words: © Shirley Erena Murray. Tune: ANZAC 2005.

Could be read or sung with appropriate permission.

The Wesley Saga

A fun reading suitable for any Wesley Celebration

Four male and eight female readers (youth or adult)

Characters: Samuel Senior, Samuel Junior, John, Charles, Susanna, Emily, Sukey, Molly, Hetty, Nancy, Patty & Kezzy.

• • •

Samuel Senior (1662–1735):
    I am Samuel Wesley, yes, that is my name,
    It means 'from the west' but from Dorset I came,
    Now Rector of Epworth, and not without fame,
    As Preacher and Poet I've made quite a name.
    I'm writing a book about Job and his hells,
    I've a family crest that features some shells,
    I'm critical, stubborn and very devout,
    I have a quick wit, and just sometimes, I shout.
    A long lack of money has caused me much pain,
    But Scholar and Gentleman I do remain.
    As an eager young man I looked for a wife
    Well-bred and of learning, to cherish for life.
    Susanna, the daughter of Doc Annesley
    Was a pretty nineteen when she married me.
    Neat and well organised for me she will care,
    I'll give her a baby – yes, one every year.

Susanna: 'Tis true, that he did, for the next nineteen years,
    And he changed no nappies, nor mopped any tears.
    Though our family was large it didn't break me
    For I had my methods of 'strict priority'
    Fear the rod and cry softly, be kind, be clean,
    And eat what you're given with nothing between.
    I taught them all reading, history and lit.
    And hubby helped out with the classics, a bit.
    The three boys won places to good public schools,

The Wesley Saga

> My girls are well read and know the grim rules
> Like, regardless of want, males must feed,
> The female role is to rise above need.
> I fear that I may be ahead of my time,
> I think about politics, views that are mine.

Samuel Senior: It is an affront, my wife dares disagree
> With my bumbling curate, and even with me!
> She started a prayer group while I was away,
> Dozens of folk met in her kitchen to pray.
> My curate's upset, made him quite venomous
> I think she's becoming some kind of feminist!

Samuel Senior & Susanna: Though sometimes we differ and often lack coins,
> We both can rejoice in the fruit of our loins.

Emily: We girls don't appear in the history books
> Yet seven of us lived, and we had more than looks.

Sukey (1695–1784): The day we turned five, A to Z did recite,
> Though Nancy took two days to get it quite right.

Molly (1696–1734): The Long Catechism we all could relate,
> Our Hetty read Greek by the time she was eight

Hetty (1697–1750): Our education was of excellent quality
> Each day, like the boys, six hours of equality.

Nancy (1701–?): Methodically trained, we could, sing, sew and spell
> Yes, whatever we did, we did very well.

Patty: Gloves knitted by Molly have lasted forever,
> The women of England keep them as a treasure.

Kezzy: We learnt to fear God and respect one another,
> And for one hour a week we each talked with Mother.

All: Alas, we were tutored beyond our calling
> And the men we married were quite appalling.

John (1703–91): I am child fifteen, second son to survive
    It's by pluck and God's grace that I am alive;
    They Christened me John then all called me Jack,
    I had a bed of my own, up top at the back
    Misfortunes were many but when just five years
    Our house caught on fire, I was trapped up the stairs.
    The others got out leaving me to expire,
    But a ladder of men snatched me from the fire.
    'Saved for a purpose' went my mother's learning
    Naming me then 'The brand plucked from the burning.'
    As a sober young man I thirsted for truth,
    With passion and purpose, the ideals of youth.
    My aim when at Oxford was to live a pure life
    Not easy, for sin was incredibly rife.
    I started my day with devotions at four,
    Then wrote and studied 'til ten pm or more.
    A position of don was very soon gained,
    But my desire was to become ordained.
    I went back to Epworth as curate for Dad,
    It helped him a bit, and it made Mother glad.

Charles (1707–88): I'm young brother Charlie, the musical one,
    With curls and good humour, and keen to have fun.
    I like folks around me so started a club
    For chaps who like church more than time at the pub.
    We visit the prisons and comfort the needy
    And pray for the souls of the rich and the greedy.
    Most students at Oxford prefer to play games
    So our Holy Club got called many rude names.
    But the tag Methodist did not worry me
    I wrote hymn 204 after hymn 203.
    We build up each other, the best way to thrive
    Good words for a hymn, see MHB number 745.
    I praised God for all things from daisies to cows
    So it seemed the right thing to take holy vows.

Samuel Junior (1690–1739):
>This was the time that Pilgrims crossed the ocean
>And my young brothers had a missionary notion.
>I Samuel Junior, respecting of tradition
>tried to prevent such un-high church ambition.
>But, converting Redskins seemed so romantic
>That soon both were preaching across the Atlantic.
>I was aghast but Mother was delighted,
>Nothing could be done so I didn't get excited.
>Priest and Headmaster is my fine vocation
>Not pearls before swine in some heathen location.
>Yes, their mission failed. It is sad to relate,
>Each returned home in a desolate state.

John: In May '38 when most wretched and down
>I dragged myself off to a meeting in town.
>In Aldersgate Street about quarter to nine,
>A soul was converted, and that soul was mine!
>While hearing the lesson around eight forty five
>My heart strangely warmed, I felt truly alive!
>I sought brother Charles, he too was a-fired,
>We burst into song, both reborn inspired.

John & Charles: Now filled with the Spirit, we're really aglow
>And both of us rearing to get up and go.

John: We preached faith and virtue…

Charles: and did it with flair.

John: We taught in the pulpits…

Charles: and in the fresh air.

John: Although small in size we were giants of our time…

Charles: And for fifty odd years we remained in our prime.

John: We started class meetings…

Charles: trained clergy and lay…

John: And travelled by horse…

Charles: a large circuit a day.

John: The world is my Parish…

Charles: our John would exclaim,
   Bringing help and salvation to the poor and the lame.

John: We spread the good news…

Charles: and we never slept long…

John: But wherever we went…

Charles: we praised God in song.

John & Charles: Though staunch C of E we two vicars remained
   Our Methodist movement could not be contained.

All: The people called Methodist spread and they grew,
   A parish world-wide that includes me and you.

Samuel Senior: Three cheers for the Wesley heritage of today…

Susanna: And all sincere Christians…

Samuel Senior: Hip, hip…

All: Hooray!

• • •

Production suggestions

- Characters simply stand in a line and step up to the microphone in turn.
- Costume: large name tags hung round necks, plus hats and aprons for the women.
- Full cast of 12 but can be performed by six or seven people: four males and two or three females… Susanna and one or two daughters reading alternately
- Susanna holds up a name tag for each girl.

How Lay Preaching Began

Ideal for Lay Preachers' Sunday, 2nd Sunday in August.

Leader: The year is 1742. The Location is The Foundery, City Road, London, headquarters of the Methodist movement. Susanna Wesley, widowed for seven years, now lives with her son John. Not that he spends much time there. Susanna sits in an armchair reading.

John: *(Unseen)* See to my horse. She suffers from a long ride. Urgent business presses upon me.

Susanna: (to herself): I expected him to be in a mood.

John: Mother! Mother! Where are you?

Susanna: Welcome home John. How good to see you. I thought that you had intended to stay in Bristol until the end of next week.

John: Something shocking was reported to me. I had to return immediately to find out the true facts for myself. You must tell me exactly what happened.

Susanna: My dear son, we can't talk now you look exhausted. You go and freshen up while I make us a nice cup of tea. It so happened that I made some special cakes yesterday – it is wonderful being able to afford occasional little luxuries. I am so proud of you John.

John: But Mother I need to know…

Susanna: No buts John, I will not enter into discussion with any man who has not washed after riding.

While we wait for the tea to draw do sample this new recipe from the book Patty gave me. They are currant and rosewater Queen cakes, dusted with icing sugar.

John: They look attractive.

Susanna: Have as many as you like Jacky.

John: Mother, you know I exercise moderation in all things. This delicacy is tasty, but I won't have another just now. I am sorry if I spoke imprudently when I arrived. I was greatly exercised by the singular news received four days ago. It appears a travesty has occurred in my chapel.

I was appalled and humiliated to receive such information. You know how important it is to follow correct protocols in worship. To act otherwise borders on blasphemy!

Susanna: You haven't told me the nature of this rumoured travesty.

John: But surely you know! Thomas Maxwell, whom I entrusted charge of the Foundery Society has usurped sacred office without being called to it. I left clear instructions that on Sundays as well as reading the lesson for the day at the lectern he may also read Mattins from the Book of Common Prayer. But I heard he had the audacity to ascend the steps to the pulpit and preach a sermon. For a mere lay man to think he could preach his own thoughts from the pulpit is not only unprecedented, but also outrageous! Please tell me it didn't happen.

Susanna: I cannot deny that this happened.

John: Oh, the disgrace…

Susanna: Once I would have considered it improper behaviour, but times change. New circumstances may dictate new ways of behaving. Think back Jacky to when you were a little boy, and your father was on one of his long visits to London. He left the parish in the care of a curate who had no aptitude for his calling. All Mr Inman ever did was lead but one service a Sunday. All his sermons were on 'sin' that he defined as not paying your debtors. Considering our impoverished circumstances, I did not want my children continually exposed to these sermons, so I decided to take a Sunday prayer meeting for the family round our kitchen table.

John: How could I forget; they were amazing times! But it wasn't just our family there were crowds of people, so many that despite standing close together they couldn't all fit in our kitchen.

Susanna: It began as a simple time of prayer for our household. We read the Bible, prayed together and I read one of your father's sermons. However, young Simon who helped with our glebe told his parents and they asked if they could join us, then so did others. Church attendance had fallen to around 25 regulars yet 200 villagers would assemble at the rectory on a Sunday. The curate complained. Your father wrote to me and demanded that if I persisted in this particular behaviour, I must have man read his sermons. I replied there was not one man among the villagers who could read a sermon without having to spell out many of the words. I believed I was doing God's will and I would continue to read his sermons until he returned.

John: You quite changed the bad attitude that many had towards our family. The people village began to look upon you as their mother.

Susanna: All I'm asking is that you talk with Thomas Maxwell and hear him preach.

John: But he's not an ordained clergyman.

Susanna: That is so, and you must judge for yourself. But I believe he is as surely called of God to preach as you are. Son, there was a time when you declared open air preaching to be vile, yet you brought the Lord's word to a crowd of 3,000 souls at Brickfields outside Bristol. That was in April 1739. Have you not continued saving hundreds of souls by open air preaching ever since? You are not going to find enough clergy to continue your great mission to the poor without the help of lay people.

John: So much needs doing. Saving souls is paramount but the minds and bodies of the poor are also greatly in need of nourishment. I have commissioned local helpers in these tasks.

Susanna: You were elected as a Fellow of Lincoln College in Oxford not only for your academic abilities but for the skill you showed teaching students. You are more than capable of training good lay men to be good local preachers.

John: It is a revolutionary thought, but it may be possible. There would have to be strict rules in regard to personal worthiness, rigorous educating and testing, and continuing accountability.

Susanna: This must be so. Leading a service of worship and interpreting God's Word is surely the highest calling of all. It requires utmost dedication and a lifetime of continual learning.

John: Mother, you are describing yourself! Your life whole life has been dedicated commitment to our Lord. Every day you methodically pray and read the Bible. You also read many other books and keep expanding your knowledge and learning new skills … maybe in times to come, even some women may become preachers!

• • •

Production suggestions

This short play reading begins with Susanna sitting in a chair reading a book *(other props include another chair and a small table on which Susanna later serves tea and cakes)*.

Noises off stage indicate an arrival of a horse and rider *(horse hooves can be made with halved coconut shells)*. John' first words are shouted from off stage.

When presenting in church keep it simple. Susanna stands at the lectern or sits at a table wearing a microphone while the person leading the service explains the setting from the pulpit. John shouts his opening words from the top of a side aisle then joins Susanna at the lectern or table.

Susanna's later years

Only 10 of Susanna's 19 children survived beyond infancy. Following the death of her husband Rev Samuel Wesley on 25 April 1735, Susanna had to leave the rectory at Epworth. Initially she and her youngest child, Keziah, lived in Gainsborough with her eldest daughter Emilia and helped with the small school she had established. When Emilia (also known as Emily) married, Susanna and Kezzy moved south to live with her eldest child, Samuel, who was Master of Blundell's School in Tiverton. From there they moved to Fisherton near Salisbury and lived with daughter Patty. In 1740 Susanna moved to The Foundery in London where John had established the headquarters of his movement. Two years later Emilia's marriage failed, and she came to live with her mother. They both supported John in his work. Susanna died at the Foundery on the 23 July 1742 surrounded by her remaining children apart from Charles who was in North Wales and could not be contacted. Three of her adult children, Molly, Sammy and Kezzy had predeceased her. Susanna was buried in Bunhill Fields, a Dissenters Cemetery opposite the Foundery. A memorial pillar stands in the grounds of Wesley's Chapel.

The Foundery

The Foundery originally supplied cannons for the nearby Honourable Artillery Company but closed in 1716 after an explosion that killed 17 men. Wesley purchased the City Road site in 1739 and converted the derelict building into a chapel that could accommodate 1,500 people plus living accommodation for himself and others. The Foundery complex provided a free dispensary that opened in 1746 with an apothecary and a surgeon. The following year also housed a free school with two masters teaching 60 children, and in 1847 opened an alms house on an adjacent section.

John Wesley's architecturally designed chapel and townhouse were built on the site between 1777-1779. Wesley lived in the house for the last twelve years of his life and died there. Household servants lived on the premises. The house was also used to accommodate travelling preachers. This continued after Wesley's death until the 1900s when it was turned into a museum. The chapel has a grade 1 listing as an example of Georgian architecture. It still functions as a church and is known as "The Mother Church of World Methodism."

Lay Preachers

Lay preaching became an essential integral part of the Methodist Movement and continues as such. The first Methodist Conference was held at the Foundery in June 1744. John invited only ten representatives to attend what he called, "A Conversation, where every person may speak freely of everything that is in his heart. And that every question that is proposed be fully debated and bolted to the brain." Six were ordained Anglican clergy plus four trained assistants or local preachers (Thomas Maxwell, Thomas Richards, John Bennett and John Downes).

The term "local preacher" is still used in England and was used in New Zealand until early in the 20th century. Until recent years it was a requirement of all Methodists seeking ordination to have first passed the lay preachers' exams and proved themselves as competent preachers by a critiquing team. To obtain a lay preacher's certificate also required being examined with oral questions by the Synod.

Ongoing training is obligatory for all who wish to retain active preaching roles. Current training requirements can be found on the New Zealand Methodist Church website and the New Zealand Lay Preachers' Association website. Trinity Theological College offers Lay Preaching courses. Non certificated local Worship Leaders may be trained within the local parish to the requirements set by that parish.

Go and Tell

A reflection on the Woman of Samaria, John 4:4-43

Cast and personalities:
Leah – leader; Lois – curious; Ruth – judgemental;
Lydia – observant; Woman of Samaria

Scene: Four women carrying water jars *(cardboard shapes with the script clipped to the back)* walk towards a well *(could be constructed from a large cardboard carton, or just a simple drawing).*

Leah: Someone has left their water jar here.

(All move closer and group around the well, facing the front, Lois looks in the jar)

Lois: It hasn't even been filled.

Ruth: How careless!

Lydia: Why would anyone leave their jar at the well?

Leah: It is a mystery, but we better get on with the job. I wish this lid wasn't so heavy.

Lois: Look who's coming!

Ruth: The brazen hussy! How dare she come at this time! The mid-day heat is all she's fit for.

Lydia: She knows respectable women don't mix with her type.

Woman of Samaria: Good evening ladies. I've come to get my jar.

(The women turn away muttering similar statements to the above.)

Woman of Samaria: I know you don't expect to see me here … but wouldn't you like to know why my water jar is here?

Ruth: If you couldn't get the lid off by yourself, don't expect us to help you.

Woman of Samaria: I can manage this lid on my own. I do it every day.

Lois: Well, why is your empty jar here?

Woman of Samaria: I've had the most amazing experience. When I arrived at my usual time there was a man here and he asked me to give him a drink.

Lydia: You always were the obliging sort when it comes to men.

Woman of Samaria: Even though we played together as children, you don't know me at all. This man wasn't a Samaritan, but he knew who I was, not my name, but who I really am.

Ruth: Your reputation sure has spread!

Woman of Samaria: I know what you think Ruth. And you are so wrong. He was a decent man and a Jew.

Leah: But Samaritans don't have dealings with Jews.

Woman of Samaria: That's what I said, Leah. I was very surprised that he even spoke to me. Then I noticed he didn't have anything to draw water with and I though he must be really thirsty. But no, he wasn't thirsty. He said he had water, special water, 'living water' he called it. He said whoever drinks this water would never be thirsty again. And then I realised he was a prophet.

Ruth: *(Sarcastically)* You looked into his eyes, deeply, I imagine.

Woman of Samaria: Yes, Ruth, I did. And I saw something I have not seen in a long while, I saw compassion. But it was unsettling … the man said I should go and get my husband. My heart thudded but his eyes were so kind I held my gaze and I told him plainly I don't have a husband. But this man knew that I was not living with my husband!

Lois: We all know that.

Woman of Samaria: He not only knew, but he also understood why. I am not ashamed of my life.

Lydia: Tell us more … please.

Woman of Samaria: Looking into those eyes I knew I was drinking that 'living water' and it was filling my body with joy. I had no need to ashamed. We talked about my first husband dying leaving two children, me marrying his brother and having four small children when he died and how I had another to the uncle who wanted a son but didn't want me.

Lydia: Caring for five children without a man would be hard.

Woman of Samaria: He understood how hard. After all my close relations had died there was a man who said I could live with him. What he wanted didn't include the inconvenience of children.

Leah: I'm sorry we were so quick to judge. *(Others nod and murmur reluctant agreement.)*

Woman of Samaria: Now, having met the prophet I feel free – free to be the person I really am – a loving and a confident woman. When the prophet's friends arrived with food, they were surprised to see me having this deep conversation with their leader. But he kept talking to me.

Ruth: Remarkable!

Woman of Samaria: He said it didn't matter if people worshiped God on this sacred mountain or in the holy city of Jerusalem. He said the important thing is to worship God in Spirit and in truth. I understood what he meant. It was a revelation an epiphany! It came to me that he might be the promised one, the messiah.

(Ruth and Lois roll their eyes and shake their heads disparagingly).

Leah: So, why did you leave your water jar?

Woman of Samaria: Well, and this is amazing, He said, 'Go and tell.' Immediately I felt I had to share this source of 'living water' with others. So, I rushed to the city gate where the men were sitting in the shade of the wall as they do in the middle of the day. I felt so different and confident that I was able to speak to them and convince them to see this man for themselves.

Lois: I heard my Samuel talking about this man to our neighbour Dan. He said there is a prophet in town who is speaking in the market place tomorrow.

Ruth: Who would have thought a woman would be listened to by men.

Woman of Samaria: The men did listen and then they went and saw for themselves.

Lydia: That is truly amazing.

Woman of Samaria: The man I met, right here at this well has changed my life forever.

Lois: Could he change ours?

Woman of Samaria: He already has. You haven't spoken to me in years. Few women have. It's like I don't have a name. But I haven't forgotten your names. And what's more I believe I have been chosen by God to talk to you – Leah, Lois, Lydia and Ruth.

Leah: You are a strange person for God to choose. But the Holy Stories often speak of God choosing unlikely people. Our Father Jacob did some dubious things, yet God used him mightily. What do you think God wants you to proclaim?

Woman of Samaria: Just this: God loves everyone regardless of who they are, what they are, or what they have done. God understands everything and is always with you. You don't have to be important to tell this news. You just have to share your story.

Lydia: Your story is amazing. I wouldn't be surprised if you are remembered for a very long time, even if your name isn't.

Lois: Are all lives important?

Woman of Samaria: They are … I'm sure of it! When I looked into the prophet's eyes, I could see he loved me – not in a man woman way – but in the way we love our children. Don't you love each one of your children? Even when they do things you don't like you still love them. You can't protect your children from everything or give them everything they want, but you keep on loving them.

Leah: Listening to others and hearing their stories can be life changing.

Woman of Samaria: The 'living water' of God's compassion is for everyone.

Lois: But how can everyone know this?

Lydia: We can't tell everyone, but we can share what we know with people we meet.

Ruth: Working together would make it easier.

Leah: Let's get the lid off this well.

(All working together lift the lid and draw water, to background music of 'Go, tell it on the mountain…' or the women sing the chorus 'Never Thirst Again')

• • •

A Peace Presentation

Requires a Worship Leader and two, three or four female readers
(If four monologues are too long for your service, make a selection)

• • •

Worship Leader: The Decade to Overcome Violence abounded with good intent, yet it brought more violence into our living rooms than any previous decade. It is easy to feel helpless in the graphic face of mass evil. Yet never before in the history of the world have there been so many people creatively working for peace. Key peace projects in to a computer and Google produces millions of references. Thousands of children are folding paper cranes, hundreds of young-people are uniting in cross-culture enterprises, numerous workers are giving their skills in causes of education, health, law enforcement, building and reconstruction. There are seminars, camps, and massive marches; Government ventures, International ventures and NGOs working tirelessly for the cause of peace. Millions of dollars are fed into the dream.

Daily, since liturgies began, priests have prayed 'Grant us peace in our time O Lord.' Every minute of every day ordinary people are praying for peace. It is easy to think there is no practical way to support these prayers. It is easy to think the actions of individuals are too insignificant to count. Yet every act of violence, and every act of peace, begins with the actions of an individual. Each kindly act, no matter how small, is a contribution to a culture of peace. Individuals have the power to work wonders.

Listen as four (or two) women share their stories. Two (or one) come from the scrolls of Hebrew Scriptures and two (or one) from the pages of New Zealand history. All are ordinary women living in their own domestic situations. Only time separates them from us. By wit and will each was a peace achiever…

Achsah (Judges 1:12–15; 3:7–11)

Abigail (1 Samuel 25:1–42; 2 Samuel 3:3)

Mary Martin (1817–84)

Hūria Mātenga (1841–1909)

• • •

Link between the reflections

Leader: This woman in her time and her place made a difference. This woman used initiative and courage. This woman gave others reason to be grateful.

Response: We give thanks for the life of… (Achsah; Abigail; Mary Martin; Hūria Mātenga)

Ending

Worship Leader: We have heard four women share their stories. Two from the scrolls of Hebrew Scriptures and two from the pages of New Zealand history, ordinary women living in their own domestic situations. Only time separates them from us. By wit and will each was a peace achiever. By wit and will we too can be peace achievers.

All sing: Let there be peace on earth and let it begin with me…

• • •

Achsah (Judges 1:12-15; 3:7–11): I am Achsah (Ak-sa) daughter of Caleb. The bravery of Caleb is legendary. In his youth he was the one selected by Moses to represent the tribe of Judah in spying out the Promised Land. It was a daunting task. Ten of the chosen declared the mission impossible. Only my father and Joshua of Ephraim stood resolute, determined that with God anything is possible. But the verdict of the ten meant all the people of Israel were doomed to wander in the wilderness for 40 years. Of that entire generation only Joshua and Caleb, were given the privilege of entering the Promised Land.

Conquering cities is a beastly business. I would have preferred to live the nomadic life I was born into, but my father said I was born to something better. He was zealous in doing what he believed to be God's will. Personally, I can't accept such a God and I wonder if our leaders have got it right. But of what account are the thoughts of a woman! A more pressing problem is the age of my father. Conquering cities is all very well for the young but it isn't something a man can do indefinitely. My father has decided to encourage would-be conquerors. He is offering a prize to the one who takes the city of Kirathsepher. 'What is the prize father?' I asked.

'Land of course,' he replied, 'but finding the right patch is a problem. The offer needs to be tempting.' He glanced briefly in my direction then back again. It was if he was seeing me for the first time in a long while. My cheeks coloured under his gaze. 'Daughter,' he said at last, 'I have found a prize worthy of the bravest warrior.'

As you can imagine I took a keen interest in that particular battle. The victor happened to be a man I knew well – my cousin Othniel. It was more than I dared hope Othneil is an imposing figure known for his honour. I sensed that he was happy with his prize. In fact, so keen was he to have me wed he didn't bother to check out the land gift. When I saw this prize, my spirits dropped. There was plenty of land but no water. I couldn't believe the foolishness of my father. Did he really expect Othneil to settle for barren land? I hoped it was an honest mistake, but I feared my husband would think otherwise.

I had come into this marriage with delight but now only trouble stretched before me. Othneil would not suffer an insult of this magnitude. He would surely take up arms against my father. Only death could come of such a feud. Othneil was still

A Peace Presentation

too captivated by his first prize to notice all was not well. I had to act quickly. I told him that although I loved him dearly, I had been smitten with homesickness.

'Let me return just for a day' I begged, 'I have a burning desire to speak with my parents and there are some things I need. Grant me this and I will not leave you again.' 'Your every wish is my desire,' he replied.

I mounted my donkey and went straight to my father's field. I dismounted before him. His eyes carried the shifty look of apprehension, but his words were strong, 'Daughter what is your wish?'

'Father,' I replied, 'I have come for a blessing. The land you gifted to my husband and myself contains no water source. Could you find it in your heart to extend the gift to land containing a spring?'

His brow slowly smoothed. 'Daughter your wish is wise. Tell your husband you can have both the upper and lower springs of Negeb.'

Two springs – did the gift reflect love or guilt? 'You are truly a generous father,' I responded.

Family harmony prevailed, but alas the people of Israel fell into evil ways, and God allowed them to be sold into the hand Cushan-rishathaim king of Mesopotamia. When the people repented and called out for a deliverer God raised up my husband as that deliverer. Othniel defeated the King of Mesopotamia and became the first Judge over Israel. His rule of peace lasted for 40 years.

• • •

Abigail (1 Samuel 25:1-42; 2 Samuel 3:1-5): My name is Abigail. My fate was to marry a surly, bad-tempered man. My parents were happy with the match as the man was very wealthy. 'You have been blessed with great beauty,' my father said with pride. I saw this blessing as a curse. Not only was the man much older than me his name was Nabal, which can translate to fool. My mother added words too soft for father to hear. 'You have also been blessed with great understanding.' With due ceremony (it cost my parents a fortune) I was packed off to Nabal's estate at Carmel. His livestock dotted the mount like a covering of pebbles. I was told last muster totalled three thousand sheep and one thousand goats. Despite his wealth Nabal was thick as a brick. I quickly discovered how to detect his moods and disarm his anger. Compared to many women I lived well and didn't have to resort to counting sheep to get to sleep! I enjoyed the responsibility of a large household and I was able to keep up with happenings beyond household concerns.

I grieved greatly when the prophet Samuel was buried. He was the voice of reason in the land. King Saul had become eccentric to the point it was said openly he was losing his mind, but he was not willing to give up the throne. The successor had been named, David, the giant slayer. Once a favourite of the King, David had married his younger daughter, but irrationality possessed Saul forcing David to live as a fugitive. After the death of Samuel, the fugitive chose our land to set up his camp. It was frightening witnessing the strength of the rebel army. They arrived during shearing and we were in a vulnerable position, however, we were not disturbed in any way.

One day an emissary of ten men arrived at our door. They were unarmed and greeted Nabal with flattering words. 'To you who live in prosperity we bring greetings in the name of David.' I served the men with food and drink. 'Peace be to both of you,' they said, 'and peace be to your house and peace be to all that you have.' I retired to let the men conduct their business, but I saw the emissary depart in haste and was filled with foreboding. My husband spoke not a word to me but never had I seen him look so smug and stubborn.

One of the young men who had witnessed the discussion came to me in a state of great anxiety. The visitors had promised not to harm our workers and asked only to take food for their needs. That incredibly stupid husband of mine had replied, 'Who is David, who is this son of Jesse? Shall I take my bread, my water and my meat that I have killed for my shearers and give it unto men whom I know not whence they be.'

I could appreciate the man's desperation in daring to tell the story. 'Mistress, he said wringing his hands, 'those men were good to us when we were in the fields. They protected our livestock from wolves. Do something,' he implored, 'No one can speak to the master. We will all be slaughtered. The army of David is 600 strong.'

No one estimates numbers more accurately than shepherds! I moved with haste directing the servants to assemble food parcels. Within a short time, the asses were laden. I made a quick list: 200 loaves of bread, two large bottles of wine, five measures of parched corn, a hundred clusters of raisins and two hundred cakes of figs. The procession departed with haste; thankful my husband was visiting a neighbour. I mounted an ass and followed the servants. My men met David's halfway down the hillside. As I came abreast David was ranting about the fellow who had requited him evil for good. I dismounted in haste and prostrated myself before the man of might. I begged he hear the words of his handmaiden. I apologised for my husband, explaining he was bound by folly and took the blame on myself. I urged David to accept my gifts and to take whatever he required without soiling his hands by needless shedding of blood. It was a desperate move. Women do not present before warriors without invitation.

This warrior listened to my words and asked me to stand. I looked him straight in the eye even though I was inwardly quaking. I'll never forget his words – 'Blessed be the Lord God of Israel who sent you this day to meet me. Blessed be your discretion, and blessed be you, who have kept me this day from bloodguilt and from avenging myself with my own hand. Go in peace to your house, for I have harkened to your voice and to your person. I grant your petition.'

I rushed back home to find Nabal feasting with a few friends. It was lucky I had not totally depleted our larder, and most fortunate that I had not touched Nabal's wine supply. The men were drinking like kings and had become very merry. Next morning, in the sober light of day, I told Nabal what had passed, and his heart died within him. With all pompousness drained he became as a dead man and after ten days he ceased even to breathe. I had dared wonder if David may offer a condolence but dismissed the thought as silly. However, in due time a messenger came but the message was not of condolence. It was a request to consider marriage. I took five of my handmaidens and gladly joined the court of David. Now, there is peace in the land, and I have born him a son, Prince Chileab.

• • •

Mary Martin (1817–84): I never expected high adventure. I was raised respectably in a rectory at Islington. My father was rector of St Ethelburga's. My elder sister Elizabeth married a clergyman, and it was hoped that I, Mary, would be so lucky, for I was a sickly child, numbered among the 'halt and the lame.' But being an avid reader, I knew there are men who appreciate compassion and a quick mind.

William Martin, a frequent visitor to the rectory, was such a man. He was an able barrister with ambition. I never much cared for legal matters, but Mr Martin was a devout Christian, and his conversation was most stimulating. He frequently expressed surprise at my wide knowledge. His surprise turned to delight when I confessed to my favourite book being John Williams' *A narrative of missionary enterprises in the South Sea islands*. It turned out he had just been appointed to the post of Chief Justice of New Zealand. He was the very first person to hold such a post. We had many wonderful discussions about life in the South Seas – the sights to be seen, the hardships to endure, the needs of the people… I expressed some envy at the adventures that lay ahead of him. Suddenly I was whirled into a dream. Mr Martin, ten years my senior, asked me if I could possibly consider being his wife and going to that heathen country as his helpmate. There wasn't time for me to prepare for the voyage, but if a rector's daughter can't organise a speedy wedding who can! We were married on the 3rd of April 1841. I had been Mrs Martin for just four days when my William left knowing that I would join him within the year.

Eight months later, my friend Elizabeth Smith and I boarded the *Tomatim* at Plymouth. It was St Stephen's day – you don't forget a thing like that, leaving family and all you have ever known the day after Christmas. I was 24. William had instructed we pack absolutely everything needed for living. What a task – pots and petticoats, blankets and books, matches and mirrors… As health had always been a personal consideration, I packed a good stock of quinine and other medicines. It was a comfort to know Elizabeth had nursing experience. We were part of a large party that included Bishop Selwyn, his wife, Sarah, and a number of clergymen and students. We were farewelled by Edward Coleridge, a clergyman and master at Eton. I felt an immediate spiritual bond with Mr Coleridge and agreed to keep him informed of progress in the Colony. Writing letters is as agreeable to me as good conversation. There was a young clergyman on board named William Cotton who remarked, 'You never say anything which is not worth hearing,' he added, 'and you have plenty to say!' I trust it was well meant. Life on board was very plain indeed but with such company we had the compensation of opportunity for high thinking. After breakfast there were daily lessons in the native language. There was no printed Māori grammar only a manuscript vocabulary and copies of St Matthew's Gospel. But we had a walking dictionary in a Māori boy who had been sent to school in England for two years.

The *Tomatin* reached Sydney in mid-April 1842 and we sailed as soon as we could for Auckland, on the *Bristolian*, arriving on 30 May. William had been allocated a property at an Auckland bay called Taurarua. A long, low, one-storied cottage perched on a hill awaited me. There was a strip of white shelly beach. Tall flax glittered in the sunlight. To a Londoner born and bred this seemed like fairyland.

There were no roads, and we were quite dependant on the Māori for food and firewood. Fish and pork are the only meat available. We ate well enough with potatoes, pumpkins, corn cabbages and fruit. My disability proved no great handicap, I had servants to help in the house and when I had need to travel, they carried me on a makeshift litter. The frequent absence of my husband was hard to bear. My great pleasure was entertaining missionaries. Bishop Selwyn graced us with his presence on several occasions. On one visit he consecrated a burial ground with a grand outlook over the sea. In less than a month Captain Hobson, New Zealand's first Governor, was there laid to rest. Later Bishop Selwyn opened a small chapel on the site naming it St Stephen's. Sarah Selwyn, along with her children and maids, frequently took up residence with us when the Bishop was touring the country or visiting the Pacific islands.

My personal sorrow was that we had no children, but I suffered no lack of company. Our neighbour, the attorney general William Swainson, regarded our house as a second home, indeed so did the staff of St John's College. Sarah once paid me the nicest of complements, 'Mary,' she said, 'you have a talent for friendship.'

People find this new county harsh – the lack of sympathy is the most trying part of a woman's lot. A kind word costs nothing and what a difference it can make! Right from the beginning I had a continual stream of visitors. Some needed more than comforting words. Primitive living conditions make illness and injury inescapable. Even a rudimentary knowledge of medical matters can make a difference. Simple remedies are best – good food, rest, herbal poultices, fresh air, and prayer.

A Peace Presentation

I had no reason to fear the natives – do they not have feelings like ours? They came to me with the same hope of health. I regularly dispensed medicines and advice, but it was not enough. 'We need a hospital,' I said to William. 'All civilised communities should have hospitals,' was his reply, 'It would keep you occupied while I am away.'

It was the strangest of hospitals – just two rough huts and a tent made of blankets. Elizabeth proved an excellent nurse and we called on Doctor Davies when necessary. William said our makeshift huts were most likely the first hospital in the whole of New Zealand. He suggested raising finance from England for a proper building. I assisted with letter writing. It was indeed fortunate that I had maintained contact with so many good people. I knew I could rely on my good friend Mr Coleridge for support.

To think it is now 1860! So much as happened. Taurarua Bay is now known as Judges Bay. It is a fitting tribute, my William worked hard to establish just legal procedures. As for our little hospital it served the community for eighteen years. The Government opened a hospital in 1847 but patients still came to us. They preferred the less formal services offered in our cottage hospital. We could speak to the natives in their own tongue. Spiritual counsel is a key ingredient in healing. Illness is a great leveller and recovery greatly unites people. I believe our small service aided the work of God and helped foster racial harmony. Throughout my hospital days I found time to tutor many Māori girls. I look upon them as my daughters.

The land wars are a terrible setback for this country. Murder is a wicked thing, so is greed. I believe war is caused by ignorance. People need to take time to understand each other. And morals must be promoted everywhere. I have dreams of a network of training institutions for young Māori men and women, for even if Mission clergy were dotted over the land like flax bushes, they would not act upon the mass of the natives effectually. If Christianity and civilisation are to take root, a team of Māori preachers must be trained, and young women educated as good wives to assist them.

William and I have taken an interest in the work of St John's College, and St Stephen's School for Native Girls from their beginnings. Two years ago, William was appointed Inspector to Native Schools. He retired last month and last week he was Knighted for his services to the Colony. The elevation is gratifying but also amusing. I curtsey and call him Sir; he bows and says M 'lady and we have a good chuckle. When I say, he is retired, it doesn't mean doing nothing. The governors of St Stephen's have invited us to manage the school. I am delighted by the prospect. A good future for this country is dependent on good education.

• • •

Hūria Mātenga (1841–1909): At present I am known as Hūria Mātenga. It is not my birth name but what people choose to call me matters little. I know who my ancestors are. My whakapaka stretches to the Tokomaru canoe. My paternal grandfather was Te Pūoho-o-te-rangi, leader of the Ngāti Tama and a renowned warrior. But my parents are followers of the pacifist teachings of Te Whiti-o-Rongomai and Tohu Kākahi. They have proved that it is not only warriors who are fitted for leadership. My parents with their pacifist commitment to peace continue as leaders of the settled community at Whakapuaka.

In September 1858 they married me to Hemi Mātenga Wai-punahau. Hemi Mātenga is the son of Metapere Wai-punahau of Kapiti, and George Stubbs, a whaler and trader, and a substantial landowner in the Waikanae area. Our wedding was a grand affair, one that reflected the standing of our families. Christ Church, Nelson was packed with Māori and Pākehā dignitaries. It was hoped our marriage would foster continuing harmony between the races. It was a political move and although I had not yet developed passion for my husband, but I was passionate about this hope. The racial wars of the north were indeed terrible. We settled in the Nelson district.

A Peace Presentation

Hēmi and I had been married five years when an adventure befell us. The weather was stormy. My brother Eraia was with us. A couple of Hēmi's friends suggested a walk along the Whakapuaka cliffs. I joined the four men in an exhilarating walk. The salt stung our nostrils, and the wind whipped our hair. Suddenly we spotted a ship cast upon the rocks. It was a brig. The name *Delaware* was visible between the surging waves. The crew began a most frantic waving. We clambered down the cliff, but it seemed there was little we could do. It is a strange thing but many Pākehās cannot swim. The ship was breaking up, but the men would not enter the thrashing sea. The man I presumed to be the captain appeared to be giving some orders. Men were scuttling and sliding across the deck. Then the captain came to the rail holding a rope. Suddenly he flung the line towards us. It fell short. There was no time to be lost. I dived into the sea and swam towards the snaking rope. I was able to bring it to shore where my companions quickly secured it to a boulder but by this time the ferocity of the waves was such that the ship was rolling, and the line kept disappearing under the churning water. Several sailors clung to the line but would not move towards the beach. My male companions thought them foolish, but I understood their terror.

'They will all drown,' I cried, and I plunged back into the waves. I reached the foremost man but before I could guide him to the shore my husband and brother came along side. Between us we rescued all but one from that stricken vessel.

Ship wrecks are common enough, but much to my surprise this one was reported with much detail in the press. They even mentioned the fire we lit on the beach to warm the chilled sailors. The Pākehā likened me to some romantic beauty called Grace Darling who had rescued four people from a shipwreck in England in 1838. Of more meaning were the reports suggesting that at this time of armed conflict in Waikato and Taranaki our actions were an expression of common humanity between the two races. This caught the imagination of the settlers. We were presented with a government award of fifty pounds and the people of Nelson presented me with a gold watch paid for by public subscription. The men were each given a silver watch. My photograph was taken many times, and I had to pose for a painted portrait. There is talk of naming a harbour tug the *Hūria Mātenga*. It's all a bit much. We did what anyone would do, but if such publicity can promote racial harmony it is a good thing. If it makes the Pākehā happy to call me 'Grace Darling' so be it. I am assured of mana among my own people by virtue of my birth. I intend to foster the best values from both cultures.

References

- *The Holy Bible*
- *A New Zealand Dictionary of Biography*
- *The First Hospital in New Zealand* – paper by Ron Malpass 2004

Disclaimer

These reflections are as accurate as possible based on the written records, but the stories are fictional recreations and not every word can be substantiated.

Mahlah and Sisters

Adapted from the story: *Why Not?* by Jean Little of Ontario.

A play reading based on a Bible story justice issue suitable for anytime of the year.

Characters: Narrator, Zelophehad (Ze-lo-phe-had), Mahlah, Noah, Hoglah, Milcah, Tirzah, Moses, Men (all others in group).

• • •

Narrator: There was a descendant of Joseph who became widowed while wandering in the wilderness. He was left with five daughters to raise. His friends offered their comfort.

Men Friends: It is so sad that your wife has died Zelophehad. If only she had given you a son. Five daughters is a tragedy.

Zelophehad: Five daughters is not a tragedy. They are five fine girls. I have no need of a son. Mahlah, Noah, Hoglah, Milcah and Tirzah are as good as sons to me.

Narrator: His friends shook their heads sadly.

Men Friends: Daughters cost. They marry and leave home. Girls contribute nothing stable to a father's household. When we come to the land that Yahweh has promised we will have our own property and prosper. Sons are needed to fish and hunt, to plant wheat and to pasture sheep. Hired help is not the same as sons.

Zelophehad: You don't know my daughters.

Narrator: And with that Zelophehad smiled and called his daughters.

Zelophehad: Meet my daughters. They listen and learn; they question and think. Gather round girls and tell my friends what is planned when we have land.

Mahlah: I will sow the seeds and pull the weeds,
And harvest the fields and bring the yields
to the threshing floor and put the grain in barns to store.

Zelophehad: Mahlah and I spend many hours discussing how crops are raised. Tell them your plans Noah.

Noah: I will plant vines where the sunlight shines
And choose the fruit for making wine
It will be very fine this wine of mine.

Zelophehad: Noah and I spend many hours discussing how wine is made. Tell them your plans Milcah.

Milcah: Already I care for our sheep and lambs,
As shepherd I'll mate the ewes with the rams
and lead the flock to pastures green
and keep them safe from harms unseen.

Zelophehad: Milcah and I spend many hours discussing the rearing and shearing of sheep. Tell them your plans Hoglah.

Hoglah: I have learnt to pull fish from out of the rills
and know how to snare birds up in the hills
I will keep our pot full of savoury stew…

Zelophehad: There is nothing my daughters cannot do!

Narrator: Zelophehad's friends looked at the girls and scratched their heads.

Men Friends: So, four of your girls are learning male skills
but the young un' can't work fields or roam hills.

Narrator: Zelophehad smiled and looked kindly down
to the little girl hiding behind his gown.

Zelophehad: Though small and shy our Tirzah is bright.
She's bright as a star and our pure delight.
Tirzah sings and dances and makes us laugh,
She can bleat like a goat and moo like a calf.

Mahlah and Sisters

This journey has been exceedingly long
but she keeps us happy with wit and song.

Narrator: Alas, when the Promised Land was close at hand
Zelophehad died.
His daughters they cried.
They groaned their grief and wailed and moaned.

Mahlah: Our dear father is gone; how can we keep on!
I'll never get to pull weeds or plant his seeds.

Noah: Our dear father is gone; how can we keep on!
I'll never get to tend vines or make his wines.

Hoglah: Our dear father is gone; how can we keep on!
I won't be able to fish the rills or hunt in his hills.

Milcah: Our dear father is gone; how can we keep on!
It's a terrible knock. Now I won't be able to tend his flock.

Tirzah: Why not?

Narrator: The others stopped crying and stared at Tirzah.

Sisters: What did you say?

Tirzah: I said, why not?
Our father has gone and of course we are sad,
but we can still do what we learnt from our Dad.

Narrator: The girls looked at Tirzah as if she was mad.

Sisters: But we aren't boys you silly goose!
Without land our skills are no use.
Only sons can inherit their father's land,
Dying is not what our father planned.
Daughters get nothing they have to glean,
Left over grain keeps the fatherless lean.

Tirzah: Father told his friends and he told us too
There is nothing that his girls cannot do!

>   He trained us well for every task,
>   So, why don't we, simply ask?

Milcah: We couldn't!

Hoglah: Perhaps we could?

Noah: But we wouldn't!

Mahlah: But perhaps we should!
>   We cannot be the only ones
>   There must be others who haven't sons
>   Other families will suffer this plight
>   If no one speaks out for what is right.

Narrator: So Mahlah and her sisters went before Moses
>   and Eleazar and the priests and the people, and said…

Sisters: We are the daughters of Zelophehad.
>   He was a wise and wonderful dad.
>   He was a brave and caring man,
>   and land for his family was the plan.
>   That Father was son-less: when he died
>   is poor reason for a promise denied.

Mahlah: I have the skills for planting seeds
>   And have strength for pulling weeds.

Noah: I know how to tend grape vines
>   and turn plump fruit into wines.

Hoglah: I have learnt to fish the rills
>   and snare birds in the hills.

Milcah: Over our father's flock of sheep
>   Good watch is what I always keep.

Sisters: Our father taught us all he knew,
>   We know exactly what to do.

Moses: Though you request is rather odd
>   Our Yahweh is a justice God.

Mahlah and Sisters

       I must consult with him in prayer,
       For your answer you wait here.

Narrator: Moses went to speak with Yahweh and be heard.
       But young Tirzah had already had a word.

Tirzah: Dear God I know that you are near,
       Please listen to our heartfelt prayer.
       We only want what we know is right
       And we will work with all our might.
       I will cook meals from Mahlah's fields,
       And serve the wine from Noah's vines,
       I'll clean and process: Hoglah's game,
       And Milcah's spun wool will be my fame.
       I maybe young but I can work as hard as anyone.

Narrator: And Yahweh smiled at Tirzah as her father had done. The word of the Lord came to Moses thus. Let the law of the Israelites be changed. The daughters of Zelophehad shall inherit their father's land portion. Furthermore, wherever there are daughters and no sons, these daughters will come to own their father's plot, thus no family will lose its rightful inheritance.

And it came to pass that Mahlah, Noah, Hoglah, Milcah and little Tirzah got their portion of land and honoured their father's name by working it well.

Men: We never thought girl farmers would be allowed,
       But the daughters of Zelophehad have done him proud.
       Their wool, wine and bread win most of the prizes
       and their hotpot dinners are full of surprises.

Narrator: But the young men of the tribe became worried.
       They went to Moses and the priests and said…

Men: The daughters of Zelophehad are prosperous
       and far too popular, for the likes of us.
       Even foreign men with these women want to tarry.
       What will happen to their land when they marry?

Ten Plays +

Narrator: Again, Moses consulted Yahweh and got an answer.
Zelophehad's daughters must marry within their clan.
When Mahlah and sisters heard this decreed
they were, to put it mildly, a little bit peeved.

Mahlah: I don't need a husband to sew seed and weed.

Noah: I don't need a husband to turn vines into wines.

Hoglah: I don't need a husband to eat good meat.

Milcah: I don't need a husband to keep my sheep.

Tirzah: But we do need mates, well I do, any rate!
Not for providing my food or my water
but because I want to have a daughter.

Narrator: Then Moses smiled and said with a wink…

Moses: It isn't as bad as you may think.
Last count there were 52,000 in Joseph's clan
enough for you all to select a good man.

Narrator: So Mahlah and sisters did as they were bid.
And Zelophehad's name is known to this day
because his girls dared challenge what was the way.
When Zelophehad's daughters took their brave stand,
their pleading for justice enabled women to own land.
A dad was made famous by his daughters' citation.
And his girls are numbered with the greats of the nation.

• • •

Based on: Numbers 26:33; 27:1–11; 36:1–13 and Joshua 17:3–6; also 1 Chronicles.

Mahlah & Sisters (B)
The Daughters of Zelophehad

The same story told in less words, suitable for devotions at fellowships, house groups and youth groups.

• • •

Narrator: There was a descendent of Joseph from the tribe of Manasseh who died while journeying the desert under the leadership of Moses. Like all Israelites he held a steadfast hope of settling his family in the Promised Land. This man was widowed. His name was Zelophehad. He left five daughters: **Mahlah, Noah, Hoglah, Milcah, Tirzah**

Noah: You can't be serious. It's blasphemy!

Hoglah: But it isn't right, it simply isn't right.

Noah: The law is sacred.

Mahlah: The Ten Commandments are sacred. I don't think all the other laws are.

Noah: Be careful Mahlah. What if someone heard you say such a thing?

Mahlah: Think about it Noah. The laws were made to protect us. If the law can't protect us the law is failing. Our mother is dead. Our father is dead. We have no brothers. We have no uncles. We are unmarried. We have two little sisters and there is no one but us to care for them

Noah: It wasn't easy for our father raising five girls when our mother died. He had to be a mother to us as well as a father.

Hoglah: But he taught us well – female skills and male skills.

Mahlah: He also taught us to think, to learn, to question. Is it his fault he had no sons?

Noah: Of course not, it's just how things turned out.

Mahlah: Perhaps Yahweh has a purpose for us.

Hoglah: For us to be a family of female beggars!

Mahlah: I think not.

Noah: How else can we survive?

Mahlah: How would orphan sons survive?

Noah: They would inherit their father's land.

Mahlah: Our father would have received land. We are his offspring. We would work his land.

Hoglah: We would, but the law won't let us.

Mahlah: What if we could get the law changed? I've prayed about this and I believe we don't need to suffer in silence. We could take our case to Moses. We can speak. We should speak. We can tell it how it is for us and will be for others. Moses is a man of God. He will pray about it.

Noah: Who knows the ways of Yahweh?

Mahlah: Yahweh is a just God. This is a justice issue.

Hoglah: You're right Mahlah. Let's talk it over with the little ones. It is important they understand. Milcah, Tirzah! *(The girls coming running)*

Milcah: Here we are!

Tirzah: What do you want us for?

Mahlah: I have a question for all five of us. Who are we?

All: We are the daughters of Zelophehad.

Mahlah: We are, and we are five proud daughters. Who are we?

The Daughters of Zelophehad

All: We are the daughters of Zelophehad and we are five proud daughters.

Noah: We are proud daughters and capable daughters. Who are we?

All: We are the daughters of Zelophehad. We are proud daughters and capable daughters.

Mahlah: We are going to go to Moses and ask him if we can keep the land that is to be given to our father. We will tell Moses that we care for sheep and goats and know how to grow crops. We must make Moses understand that girls are as worthy as sons.

Noah: How we behave is very important. How can we make a good impression?

Hoglah: We will have to be very brave. Can you be brave?

Milcah & Tirzah: We are brave.

Milcah: We will wear our best clothes and be very polite.

Tirzah: We will be the Fearless Five.

Hoglah: We will. *(Putting her arms around the 2 little ones)* Who are we?

All: We are the Fearless Five.

Mahlah: If we succeed, all daughters without brothers will have the right to own land. We will be blessed, and we will bring blessings to others. Our story will be told and re-told. Not only will the name of Zelophehad be remembered so will the names of his five daughters.

Narrator: After praying over the issue Moses granted Zelophehad's land share to his daughters and inheritance rights for females in all families without male heirs.

In the fullness of time this came to pass. The Daughters of Zelophehad owned land and became famous. The names

Mahlah, Noah, Hoglah, Milcah and Tirzah are detailed in the books of Numbers and Joshua.

Their names appear in the census recorded in the book of Numbers. The only other females given this honour are Serah, daughter of Asher, and the mother and sister of Moses, Jochebed and Miriam. We can conclude that Mahlah, Noah, Hoglah, Milcah and Tirzah are among the most important women in the Hebrew Scriptures.

Share their story. Be empowered by their example. Speak out against injustice. Your small personal effort could help enable lasting benefits for many.

• • •

Based on: Numbers 26:33; 27:1–11; 36:1–13 and Joshua 17:3–6; also 1 Chronicles.

Christmas Women

Women talking to women, sharing encounters with Mary

A set of Meditations and Bible readings, suitable for:

- Advent Devotions *(Five female readers – omit Carols & Bible Readings)*
- Any Advent Service, or a Christmas Eve Candle-lighting Service (five female and one to five male reader/s for lessons, plus worship leader)
- A series of Advent Wreath Meditations *(Two to ten readers)*

• • •

Meditation 1 — Elizabeth (Mary's cousin) talks with Anna

Suggested Hymns:

- *Look toward Christmas!* Verses 1 & 2. See no. 30
  Carol our Christmas – New Zealand Hymnbook Trust 1996, or

- *Come thou long expected Jesus.* Verses 1 & 2. No. 200
  With One Voice – Collins 1982.

Based on Luke 1:5–13

• • •

I had a special dinner waiting for Zechariah (*KJV, Zacharias*). I was so proud of him! As you know Anna, not many small-town priests get the honour of entering the Holy of Holies. I'm so glad you saw him go in. Didn't he look fine in his robes? If only you had been there when his duties were over! He arrived home in a terrible state. He tried to tell me what had happened, but he couldn't speak – not one word could he get out. I was really worried; thought he had contracted some terrible illness. But he looked healthy enough, in fact he looked…radiant is the word that comes to mind. Well, there he was flinging his arms around and trying to mime something. This is crazy, I said, and went and got the slate.

When I read what he had written I was staggered. But then, I thought, why shouldn't my husband receive a vision. He is a good man. And he is married to a good woman. I've never believed barrenness to be a punishment for wrongdoing. Many good women have been barren – Rachel, Hannah and Samson's mother. But when Zech (*Zac*) gave my hand an impulsive squeeze reality kicked in. His knuckles are misshapen with arthritis. We are an elderly couple. Then I thought of Sarah and I clasped these worn hands in a little prayer of delight.

Zech was keen to go to bed right there and then but I wasn't having a good meal wasted. I'd put a lot of love into this dinner – his favourite food, special candles and all. Besides, Zech had walked a long way and he needed to keep his strength up.

I was pregnant within the month. I didn't dare believe it for months but deep down I knew. Well over forty and never felt fitter! Even so I was little embarrassed and kept myself well hidden. But we got a visitor. It was my cousin's girl, Mary, the one engaged to Joseph, the carpenter. She should have been at home preparing for the wedding. It was a shock seeing her. I hadn't told anyone. But she knew! She hugged me and called me blessed.

I know I can trust you Anna… the thing is the girl was pregnant. Don't breathe a word of this. It is a difficult situation – the child isn't Joseph's. Yet, when she told me she wasn't distressed. Turns out, she too had been blessed with a vision. The very moment Mary told me she was pregnant my child leapt in my womb. I'd felt little flutters before, but this was a real kick, a kick of joy. I knew it was a sign.

Mary stayed for three months. We crafted our own song of joy based on Hannah's. We did our exercises together and made baby clothes. She does exquisite work for one so young – you should see her swaddling cloths! It was a good thing Zech couldn't talk because he wouldn't have got a word in edgeways! Of course, I did feel sorry for him, especially after our son was born. He so wanted to bless him.

The child was perfect. The birth hadn't been too bad. The labour was strong but steady. The midwife said I was pushing well. Young Mary was a great help, sponging my brow, rubbing my back and clasping my hand. I was so tired but what a wonderful feeling holding my own baby. A son for Zechariah. He didn't need words to tell me he loved me.

The neighbours were all around with little gifts. They were astounded when I told them our boy would be called John. There are no Johns in your family they said. You must call him after your husband. They mean well, but really, who do they think they are!

Anyway, they pestered Zechariah asking him to nod agreement. Instead, he reached for his slate and wrote, The child's name is John. Why John, they shrugged. "John," shouted Zechariah, "is the name God has chosen." Well, that knocked them for a six, really shut them up. Zech and I just hugged each other and didn't care what the neighbours thought. We had our son. We had each other and God had lifted his punishment. Life can be wonderful Anna.

• • •

Meditation 2 — Anne (Mary's mother)

Suggested hymns:

- *Of the Father's Love Begotten.* Verses 1-3. No. 215
  With One Voice.

- *Carol our Christmas, an upside-down Christmas.* No. 7
  Carol Our Christmas

Based on Luke 1:39–45

• • •

Our Mary is a good girl – always was, always! No one could want for a better child. A beautiful baby! Right from infancy she was contented, smiled at six weeks and didn't stop. As daughters go, she was pure delight – sunny natured, helpful, thoughtful, and clever too, a dab hand at weaving. You should see her seamless garments! And there is no denying that she is maturing into a beauty. Only fifteen but Joseph, the carpenter, has been besotted with her for years. He's quite a good catch – his business is well established. He doesn't own any land. My dream was a farmer who could have lifted our circumstances, but Joseph is well thought of, a good tradesman and a good man. Yes, I know he's coming up thirty, but he is kind and considerate. What farmer has those qualities! I was happy with the match-makers choice and so was Mary.

But something went wrong. I felt it in my bones the moment I returned from the well. Mary had been crying. You can't hide the tell-tale signs from a mother. Wouldn't tell me anything! She was withdrawn for days. I didn't push it. Teenagers can be difficult. Then all of a sudden, she changed, and I mean changed, not the happy out-going child of before, she was a different person. Seemed mature, if you know what I mean, at peace with herself, yet quietly excited, as if she had a special secret. I wanted to believe it had been merely nerves and now she was reconciled and looking forward to the wedding.

Then, I saw her packing. "What is the meaning of this?" I demanded. She told me she was going to visit my cousin Elizabeth. It all came out. She had a secret alright! My fears were not idle. She was pregnant. I was pretty mad; I can tell you. "This is the very worst thing that could happen to us," I said, and she went on about angels. Said the Angel had told her Elizabeth was pregnant too. Angels indeed! Well, that did it, I let rip. After all we had done for her. We would never be able to hold our heads up again. It suited me just fine to have her out of the house. And as for Elizabeth being pregnant, the woman was forty-nine in the shade. My parting shot was, "Just you stay with old Lizzie until she has this miracle baby."

Of course, I was sorry afterwards. She is a good girl. We would have cared for her, no matter what. I'm sure she knows this. She left a letter for Joseph. The poor man was utterly distraught, but he got over it. I told you he is a good man. He says he will do what is best for our Mary. I'm going to a grandmother. Being a grandmother is not the worst thing that can happen.

...

Meditation 3 — Woman Traveller

Suggested hymn:

- *There's a light upon the mountain.* No. 207 *With One Voice.*

Based on Luke 2:1–5

• • •

Jolly silly idea if you ask me – having to travel to the town where your husband was born just to be counted. Why couldn't they count you where you are living now? You could say which tribe you are from. However, it's not every day we get to go on a journey. We are going on a holiday; I told the girls. You are going to see your grandparents.

It was no small task organising everything. I turned the children's bedrolls into bags to wear on their back with spare clothes tucked inside. Luckily mine are old enough to walk. Martha's son is heavy for a three year old. She made a sling to carry him in. Her Tim took him on his back at times. It was the girl, Mary, I felt sorry for, she was almost due. Joseph made her a stout walking stick. What she needed was a donkey, but landless people don't have donkeys.

We got quite friendly on the way. Well, you do, don't you, all travelling together. She was such a pleasant person. My girls just loved her. She wasn't worried about the birth. Said the baby would come in God's good time. Easy to tell it was her first, but far be it from me to scare a young woman. I'd helped deliver Martha's son, now that was a difficult birth, such a big baby. She's lucky to have him, the first two didn't go full time, stillborn, both of them.

When we arrived at Bethlehem the place was fair humming and quite booked out. Of course, we were going to Tim's parents. Martha and Saul had family too, but Joseph's parents had died. They intended staying at an inn. Every inn we passed had a no vacancy sign up. Mary told us not to worry. She was a calm one, that Mary – in my opinion, a woman of faith!

• • •

Meditation 4 — Inn-keeper's Wife

Suggested Hymn:

- *Once in Royal David's City.* Verses 1–2. No. 237 *With One Voice.*

Based on Luke 2:7–14

What a night! We were chocker! Not a bed anywhere. Not so much as a blanket to spare. The guests were all calling for ale. I was run off my feet. Not that I minded. This census thing is certainly good for business. It's not often Quirinius does anything useful.

Anyway, Dan had barred the door, but people kept knocking. When someone pounded with a stick Dan unbolted the door with a curse. It was lucky I was nearby because I saw these travellers. The man was supporting a young woman. She was heavily pregnant. Dan was in no mood to give directions, but I couldn't just shut the door on a pregnant woman. I moved over to tell them about the Three Mile Inn, being on the far side of town it was always last to fill. Then I saw the woman clutch her husband. She was more than merely pregnant.

I took charge. Got Dan to move a couple of horses out of the stable and tether them round the back; sent the boy to open a fresh bale of hay; we made a reasonable bed. I asked among the guests for a mid-wife and sure enough there was one. I gave her a lantern. It wasn't very dark considering it was mid-winter. Strange really as the moon was only a slender crescent. The light was coming from a star. I'd never seen this star before. But as you know I was busy. When finally, all the guests had bedded down I checked the window for another look at that star and I'll swear to my dying day that the whole sky lit up, bright as day it was, and I heard music! A moment later the mid-wife came in wanting more hot water. I blurted out, "The child's been born." "It's a boy," she said.

I took them some breakfast late in the morning. The couple were so gracious in their thanks. Lovely people – her name was Mary. You'd never guess where the baby was sleeping?

• • •

Meditation 5 — Anna (the prophetess)

Suggested hymn:

- *Born in the night.* No 642. *With One Voice*

Based on Luke 2:36–38

I am an old woman and I have seen many things. I was widowed when my son was but six years old. My daughters were one and four. But I managed. God took care of us. They grew to be fine people and have families of their own. I will be grateful all my days. It is my privilege to serve God with prayer and fasting.

I fear for this land of ours so long occupied by Rome. There is much unrest and many godless people. Yet recently I have seen signs of hope. It is my belief that a messiah will come and deliver Israel from her oppressor. I dare think that such a one has been born. I talked this over with my old friend Simeon. He listened carefully and agreed it could be. He told me that once he had dreamed, he would not die until he had seen the messiah. I believe God's spirit is with Simeon. He is a good man, a devout man, and so good with words. But he's not as quick at picking up on signs and feelings as I am. So, we wait in hope and encourage each other.

I saw the child first. I recognized the mother, Mary, kinswoman to my good friend Elizabeth. I recalled the strange connection between the pair and suddenly I just knew! "That's the child," I breathed. Simeon paused only long enough to gaze from my eyes to the child's. Understanding flooded his soul as it had mine. He took the child and praised God with the eloquence of a psalmist.

Then it was my turn. I held the blessed infant and told the surprised parents that his was no ordinary child. This child had the potential to save Jerusalem and yea, the whole world. As I gazed at the peaceful bundle, I knew the way to salvation was not by the sword. I said to all who would listen, "A new order is coming. This child is the prince of peace."

• • •

Advent Service Outline

Introduction (Leader): As we prepare for our Christmas, we invite you to reflect on the women of that first Christmas. The words of Scripture are well known. We invite you to feel behind the words to the reality of the women. Step back from the familiar traditions; consider other possibilities; open hearts and minds to receive Christ afresh.

Present the five Meditations sequence as above.

Closing (Leader): We have walked with women who have witnessed the beginning of the Christmas story. We open ourselves to new possibilities. Let us pray:

Birthing God, bringer of joy, hope, love, peace and new beginnings, keep our imaginations active and our hearts generous. Help us meet this Christmas with a deeper appreciation of all that Christmas means. Keep us mindful that the work of Christmas is never done. We offer ourselves as Christmas People. Amen

Benediction: Go into the world. Go blessed. Go to bring hope to every task you do.

• • •

Advent Service Suggestions

- Place a nativity scene at front of church as a worship focus

- Worship Leader reads from the pulpit

- The 'Christmas Women' read the meditations from the lectern (suitable headscarves add to the atmosphere)

- Bible Readers read from pews or a microphone in the body of church *(unless specifically a women's service, use male reader/s)*

- Stay with one version of the Bible. If using the King James Version (which could make a pleasing contrast to the contemporary feel of the women's stories) use names in brackets for the Elizabeth Meditation as the script names come from later versions – (Zacharias / Zac) not Zechariah, (Cyrenius) not Quirinius. Elizabeth is spelt (Elisabeth) in the King James Version.

- A solo carol or choir item may be slotted in anywhere suitable to the text.

- If using a carol that mentions a donkey you may like to explain 'the donkey' is a cherished tradition but is non biblical and it is unlikely that a landless carpenter would have a donkey.

- This prayer can be used in any Advent service:

    An Advent Prayer

    Advent has come.
    In this holy season of anticipation
    Enable us to embrace Christmas in all its fullness.
    Help us enter the magic world of myth and story
    with the unfettered imagination of a child…
    Present in the moment
    Living in the story.

    Help us meet angels in our story.
    May angels quell our fears
    as they did for Mary and Joseph;
    May angels give us safe directions
    as they did for the Magi;
    May angels startle us to wonder
    as they did for the shepherds.
    And may we be surrounded by angels…
    Uplifted by the hope and peace
    that evokes joy and promotes
    spontaneous acts of love. **Amen**

    • • •

Advent-Wreath Meditations

- Prepare an Advent-Wreath using 5 candles – place one candle at each end of an even cross with a taller 'Christ Candle' in the centre.

  Traditionally the Advent Candles are purple representing royalty for the 'Prince of Peace' or blue reminding of Mary and the sky. The 'Joy' candle may be pink (rose) accentuating the joy of this season. The Christ candle is traditionally white representing purity. If plain white candles are used for the weeks of Advent the centre candle may be red or purple.

- Circle wreath with greenery, this symbolises the cycle of the seasons and the circle the never-ending God; the greenery suggests new life.

- This sequence follows the traditional order for the Advent Candles: Hope, Peace, Joy, Love

•••

First week of Advent

Candle lighter: Elizabeth, a good woman and wife of Zechariah, knew anticipation and hopeful longing. I light this candle in the Spirit of Hope.

Elizabeth's meditation (Another voice)

•••

Second week of Advent

Candle lighter: Anne, the mother of Mary, experienced the twists and turns of parental love. I light this candle in honour of Anne and all parents who long for their children to know peace. I light this candle in the Spirit of Peace.

Anne's meditation (Another voice)

•••

Third week of Advent

Candle lighter: Un-named ordinary women supported Mary. Supporters are initiators of Joy. I light this candle in honour of all ordinary people who bring joy. I light this candle in the Spirit of Joy.

Woman Traveller and Inn-keeper's Wife (2 voices)

• • •

Fourth week of Advent

Candle lighter: Anna, a holy woman and prophet, understood love. I light this candle in honour of Anna and all holy people. I light this candle in the knowledge that love could save the world.

Anna's meditation (Another voice)

• • •

Christmas Day

Candle lighter: Mary the chosen one gave birth to Jesus. I light this candle in honour of all chosen people. I light this candle to celebrate Christ, the Light of the World.

(No meditation.)

• • •

For a Christmas Eve Candle Service

Combine the Advent Service with the Candle-lighters' words before each meditation.

• • •

An Advent Prayer

(For two voices or read antiphonally by the congregation alternating the pulpit and lectern sides of the church)

Voice 1: Prepare us now, Lord Jesus,

Voice 2: for the simple wonder of you coming among us…

Voices 1 & 2: As we reflect on your humble birth, and your radical life
may we understand what they could mean for us.

Voice 1: Are we, ordinary Christian people, that we are,

Voice 2: called to live radical lives in our time?

Voice 1: Does your birth mean us showing love to our neighbours?

Voice 2: Does your birth mean us actively working for peace?

Voice 1: Does your birth mean us giving hope to needy friends?

Voice 2: Does your birth mean us bringing joy to those we encounter?

Voice 1: Does your life mean us entering fully into life like you did

Voice 2: enjoying good things like food and drink, solitude and company, as well as being alert to injustice and greed?

Voice 1: Does honouring your life mean us caring for your world?

Voice 2: Does honouring your life mean us healing ills in our communities?

Voice 1: Does remembering you mean speaking up for those who cannot speak, supporting the troubled and the weak?

Voice 2: Does your life mean justice encompasses us?

Voices 1 & 2: If this is why you came, help us O Lord,
to move from understanding to action. Amen.

• • •

No Room

A play for Advent that promotes Christian World Service (CWS).

(Eight characters plus narrator)

• • •

Narrator: I want to introduce you to two ordinary New Zealand families.

The families come on from different sides and make a line.

Smiths – All together: We are the Smith family.

Dad: I am the father, Mr Smith. *(Bow)*

Mum: I am the mother, Mrs Smith. *(Bow)*

Talia: I am the daughter, Talia Smith. *(Bow)*

Peter: I am the son, Peter Smith. *(Bow)*

Smiths – All together: We are an ordinary family.

Narrator: And now the Jones family.

Jones – All Together: We are the Jones family.

Dad: I am the father, Mr Jones. *(Bow)*

Mum: I am the mother, Mrs Jones. *(Bow)*

Harry: I am a son, Harry Jones. *(Bow)*

Jack: I am another son, Jack Jones. *(Bow)*

Jones – All Together: We are another ordinary family.

Jones family walk off

Narrator: They are ordinary families, and they have lots of toys. The Smith children are playing in their bedrooms. Mother comes in.

Mum: Just look at this room of yours Talia – toys and books and clothes everywhere! You must clean it up and put everything away in its proper place.

Talia: Do I have to?

Mum: Yes, and right now.

Talia: But Dad said he would take us Christmas shopping. We are going to buy a present for you. Dad said…

Dad: Did I hear someone talking about me?

Talia: You said you would take us Christmas shopping.

Mum: And I said, this room must be tidy before you go anywhere.

Dad: Quite right! Tidy rooms and then Christmas shopping.

Talia: I love Christmas. I like buying presents and I like getting presents. I will get lots and lots of presents.

Mum: If you don't tidy this mess up there will be no room to fit any presents.

Dad: Christmas isn't just about presents.

Talia: Yes, it is. We get presents from Santa and presents from everyone in our family.

Dad: I wonder if your brother knows what Christmas is really about. Peter, Peter.

Peter: Yes Dad.

Dad: Do you know what Christmas is about?

Peter: Presents.

Mum: And?

Peter: *(Doubtfully)* Family – getting together for Christmas dinner.

Dad: Good. Anything else … someone's birthday?

No Room

Peter: The baby Jesus. It's his birthday!

Mum: Well done Peter! The wise men gave presents to the baby Jesus. We can't give presents to Jesus, so we give presents to our family.

Peter: I was in a play about Jesus. I was the man who owned the hotel, but they called it an inn. I had to say, 'No room at the inn.'

Talia: Why did you have to say that?

Peter: Because Mary and Joseph need a place to stay. She was going to have a baby and there was no room for them. The inn was full up. The only place they could stay was in the cowshed round the back with the animals.

Talia: That's awful. Did they have to sleep with cows?

Peter: Not only cows, all sorts of animals, goats, hens, donkeys… There probably wasn't much room in the shed either.

Talia: Yuk, it would be smelly and dirty.

Peter: And dark. It was night time. They didn't have electric lights or even battery torches in those days.

Talia: It would have been horrible and scary.

Mum: Yes, I would think Mary would have been very scared giving birth to a baby in a place like that. I know I would have been. Babies need a lot of care. It was certainly not safe being surrounded by animals and germs.

Talia: But Jesus was a very special person. I think it is really sad that he had to be born in a cowshed. I'm glad I was born in a nice clean hospital.

Dad: Speaking of clean and tidy places. What does your room look like Peter?

Peter: It all tidy, except for my Playmobile (or Lego). I'm making a big building.

Dad: OK but pack up the pieces you aren't using.

Scene change

Narrator: The Smith children like making things. The Jones boys are a little older. They like electronic toys and the computer.

Jack: Hey, Harry. I just googled 'Christmas' and look what came up, a place called Christmas Island. It should be a fun place.

Harry: *(Reading)* History – Captain William Mynors of the *Royal Mary*, named the island when he sailed past it on Christmas Day in 1643. It is now owned by Australia…

Jack: Skip that boring stuff, let's click on the images.

Harry: It all photos of boats crammed with people. There's no room to move on those boats.

Jack: Look, this one has sunk. A rescue boat is getting people out of the water.

Dad: Hullo boys, what are you looking at?

Harry: It's a shipwreck at a place called Christmas Island.

Jack: I thought Christmas Island would be a nice place, but this doesn't look nice. Do you know what happened to this boat Dad?

Dad: Yes, I do. I'm afraid that despite its name Christmas Island is not a nice place at all. Boats crossing that water are often not seaworthy. They have too many people on board and sometimes they sink.

Harry: But why Dad? Who are the people, are they going on holiday?

Dad: No, these are desperate people – people who can't get work and they can't feed their families. Some of them have been treated very badly. They have nowhere to live in their own countries. They are trying to find a safe place to live.

Jack: But where do they come from and where are they going?

Dad: They are Asian people, from poor countries above Australia. We call them boat people because they get on boats to go to Australia. They think they will be safe there. They think they will be able to get work and look after their children properly.

Harry: So, what goes wrong?

Dad: Everything. The boats aren't safe. The people they pay are smugglers – bad people who take large amounts of money from them and make promises that are untrue. The smugglers don't care, they only want to make money. Australia won't have these people.

Jack: Why not? Australia is a big country with lots of space.

Dad: True but finding work for everyone isn't easy and it costs a lot of money to build houses, schools and hospitals. The Government says there is no room for them. The boat people don't understand this. Those who don't drown trying to get to Australia are intercepted.

Jack: What does that mean?

Dad: It means the boats are stopped before they arrive in Australia and the people are taken to Christmas Island. I'll see if I can find some pictures of what it is like on Christmas Island.

Harry: High wire fences. Is it a prison?

Jack: There are tents in this picture, big tents. Are they having a camping holiday?

Dad: This is what it's like inside those tents.

Harry: Bunks, all crammed together.

Jack: There's no space, no room. What do they do with their things?

Dad: All they own is kept in plastic bags under the bunks.

Jack: I can't see any toys. Don't they have any children there?

Dad: Yes, they do have children there, but these kids don't have toys. They don't even have a place to play inside the wire compound.

Harry: Do they go to school?

Dad: Yes, it says here they have a school. It's not a very good school but it keeps the children occupied for a few hours a week. And at times they are taken outside the wire to a field where they can kick a ball around, but most of the time they live in very cramped conditions.

Harry: What do they eat?

Dad: Rice is the main food, often plain rice with nothing else. There isn't even room for them to all sit at tables. Many have to sit on their bunks to eat. Life is very bleak and sad. People can stay there for years while the Australian Government decides what to do with them.

Jack: I bet our Government wouldn't turn away desperate people and lock them up like that. We are better than that.

Dad: Ah, well, so far, no boat people have managed to get to New Zealand, but our Government is worried that they might. So worried, our government is making a law to stop them. They say there is no room here.

Harry: But that's not true we could make room and so could Australia. I wish there was something we could do to help those poor people. It must be awful being a kid living like that.

Dad: I don't know of any way we can help these people only Australians can do that. All we can do about boat people is to ask our Government not to be like Australia. But there are other places where children live in terrible conditions. And there are things we can do to help them.

Jack: We've got lots of toys we never use because we are too old for them. There's my small bike with the trainer wheels and the expanding plastic goal post and lots of things. We could pack them up and send them to kids who don't have any toys. Our old toys could be their Christmas presents.

Dad: That's a kind thought Jack but not practical, I'm afraid. It costs too much to send large toys off to other countries. Besides what very poor kids need most is good food and to have good food their parents need work that will provide food.

Jack: Well, we can't help with that.

Dad: Ah, but we can. I think your Mum might have some ideas, see if you can find her Jack:

Mum: You are all looking serious. How can I help?

Harry: We want to know how we can help kids who are very poor and won't get any presents at Christmas.

Mum: What a lovely idea. There are lots of things we could do. Some people fill a shoebox with presents and they are delivered to children in who live in poor countries. The Christmas shoeboxes have to be done in October to be distributed in time.

Harry: It is December now.

Mum: Yes, but we can still give money to help poor families make a better life for themselves. Let me show you the Christian World Service website. Here it is CWS Christmas Appeal. CWS helps these people with money given by people like us. Our money can really change their lives.

Dad: Isn't there a scheme where instead of us giving presents to people who don't need them, we can use that money to buy something for a family who needs help just to live?

Mum: Yes, look at this, Gifts – the joy of giving. We could buy bees or a hen, or a goat. Your uncles and aunts don't need the presents we buy them, these people do.

Jack: But our uncles and aunts would think we had forgotten them.

Mum: No, they wouldn't because if we gave money to buy these special gifts, we would get a card that says what each gift is. We give that card to the person we didn't buy a present for, then that person knows they have helped do something worthwhile this Christmas.

Harry: These gifts aren't presents that kids can give because we don't have that much money.

Dad: Well, you do have toys you don't need, unwanted stuff can be turned into cash you know.

Jack: Yes! Yes! We could sell toys on Trade Me.

Harry: We could keep some of the money and give some away.

Dad: Great idea boys!

Scene change. Jones family move off. Smith family move on.

Narrator: Meanwhile, back at the Smith's house the Smith children have arrived home from their Christmas shopping.

Dad: We just got home in time. Listen to that rain. I'll put these presents away for now, we will wrap them tomorrow. You kids play in your rooms for a while.

Kids: Yes Dad. Thanks for taking us shopping.

Talia: What are you making with your Playmobile. Peter?

Peter: It's a hotel like where we are going to stay after Christmas.

Talia: It could be the inn where there was no room for Jesus. We can fill it up with Playmobile (or Lego) people. They can be eating and drinking and sleeping.

Peter: OK. I'll finish the building you find the people and things.

Mum: Those kids have been very quiet for a long time.

Dad: Yes, I think we should see what they are up to.

Mum: You kids look busy. What are you making?

Peter: It is the inn that Mary and Joseph went to.

Talia: See it's all crowded. There is no room for them. I feel sad no one made room for them and the baby.

Dad: When I was a boy, we always put a nativity scene under our Christmas tree.

Peter: What's a nativity scene?

Dad: Nativity means birth. It is a model of Mary and Joseph and the baby in the stable with the animals and shepherds and wise men.

Mum: Well, you have done a really beautiful job of this. I think we should take it into the lounge. We can put it on a little table beside the Christmas tree to remind everyone that Christmas is really about making room for Jesus.

Talia: Then we can make a nativity scene.

*Smiths go off; all return line up, bow,
and uncover a nativity scene and the crowded inn.*

The Jones family could be holding CWS advertising material.

• • •

Production notes

The scene above can be done with a laptop computer as a simple prop, or as a PowerPoint slideshow so the photos the Jones' talk about appear on screen for all to see. If using a CWS Christmas PowerPoint a few words could be said about each picture, either by the family, or the narrator.

If Playmobile or Lego isn't available use any construction toy and small figures. Adapt the script to fit what you have. The Nativity set can be any Nativity that children could put together. Assemble before the service and have it up the front covered with a cloth.

Ten Plays +

The two families keep to their own sides. Each family has a table. The Jones table has chairs and laptop. The Smith table has a standing notice ('Peter's Room') that conceals the completed crowed inn model.

All the plays are intended to be read.

• • •

A Christmas Story

Option 1: 13 stick-puppets and four speakers.

• • •

Option 2: Simplified Version.

Could be presented by children, one reader for each puppet. Number of puppets may be reduced by three or four. Star, Lamb, Official and Stable are not essential.

(See page 97)

• • •

- **Speaker A:** Man, Inn Keeper, King, Star.
- **Speaker B:** Woman, Bunch of shepherds, Official, Stable.
- **Speaker C:** Baby, Lamb, Bunch of Wise Guys, Donkey.
- **Speaker D:** Angel.

• • •

[Set 1]

A: I am a man.

B: I am a woman.

C: I am a baby.

A: I am an inn keeper.

B: I am a bunch of shepherds.

C: I am a lamb.

A: I am a king.

B: I am an official.

C: I am a bunch of wise guys.

A: I am a star.

B: I am a stable.

C: I am a donkey.

D: I am an angel.

All: Together we make the Christmas Story.

[Set 2]

A: I am a man; I am a tradesman.

B: I am a woman, not much more than a girl.

C: I am a baby; I've just been born.

A: I am an inn keeper; my inn is overflowing.

B: We shepherds have to watch sheep at night.

C: I am a lamb, a very young lamb, baa.

A: I am a king, I give orders.

B: I am an official, I carry out orders.

C: We wise-guys are astrologers.

A: I am a star, I shine brightly.

B: I am a stable, I shelter animals.

C: I am a donkey, hee-haw.

D: I am an angel: I am a messenger from God.

All: Together we make the Christmas Story.

A Christmas Story

[Set 3]

A: I am a man, I am a tradesman, I work hard.

B: I am a woman, not much more than a girl, I have just become a mother.

C: I am a baby, I've just been born, this is a new beginning.

A: I am an inn keeper, my inn is overflowing, travellers are sleeping in my stable.

B: We shepherds have to watch sheep at night, we are poor and smelly.

C: I am a lamb, a very young lamb, but this night I felt something special, baa.

A: I am a king, I give orders, I am powerful and rich.

B: I am an official, I carry out orders, I am dutiful.

C: We astrologers are educated and cultured.

A: I am a star, I shine brightly, I guided the travellers.

B: I am a stable, I shelter animals, I am useful.

C: I am a donkey, hee-haw.

D: I am an angel. I am a messenger from God. The message is amazing.

All: Together we make the Christmas Story.

[Set 4]

A: I am a man, I am a tradesman, I work hard, I am an ordinary man.

B: I am a woman, not much more than a girl, I have just become a mother after making a long journey.

C: I am a baby, I've just been born, this is a new beginning, I am a new baby.

A: I am an inn keeper, my inn is overflowing, travellers are sleeping in my stable, I couldn't turn them away.

B: We shepherds are night workers, we are poor and smelly, we are marginalised people but this night we saw something special.

C: I am a lamb, a very young lamb but this night I felt something special, so special I left my mother and followed the shepherds, baa.

A: I am a king, I give orders, I am powerful and rich. My journey is to be great.

B: I am an official, I carry out orders, I am dutiful; a solider or a census scribe.

C: We astrologers are educated and cultured, and clean, despite having travelled from afar.

A: I am a star, I shine brightly, I guided the travellers. I am the brightest star of all.

B: I am a stable, I shelter animals, I am useful, I can shelter all sorts.

C: I am a donkey, hee-haw.

D: I am an angel. I am a messenger from God. The message is amazing. The story is wonderful. It's Awesome!

All: Together we make the Christmas Story.

[Set 5]

A: I am a man, I am a tradesman, I work hard, I am an ordinary man, a peasant.

D: Peasants, tradesmen, and ordinary men, are all special to God.

B: I am a woman, not much more than a girl, I have just become a mother.

D: Girls, mothers and all women are special to God.

C: I am a baby, I've just been born, this is a new beginning. I am a new baby.

D: All babies are special to God.

A: I am an inn keeper, my inn is overflowing, travellers are sleeping in my stable, I couldn't turn them away. This is a new thing for me.

B: I am an official, I carry out orders, I am dutiful whether I am a soldier or a census scribe. My journey is to do my duty.

D: People in business and people who serve are special to God.

C: I am a lamb, I am very young but this night I went on a journey, an adventure, baa.

A: I am a king, I give orders, I am powerful and rich, my journey is to be great, I don't care who I hurt in the process.

B: We shepherds are night workers, we are poor and smelly, we are marginalised people but this night we saw something special, so special we left our sheep and made a journey.

C: We astrologers are educated and cultured, and clean, despite having travelled from afar; we bring spices and gold.

B: I am a stable, I shelter animals, I am useful, I can shelter all sorts, but this night I am sheltering something very special

C: I am a donkey, hee-haw.

Ten Plays +

D: Whatever your circumstances, rich or poor, powerful or humble, leader or worker, young or old, cultured or marginalised, clean or smelly, you have a place in the Christmas story.

[Set 6]

A: I am a man who has become a father.

B: I am a woman who has just given birth.

C: I am a baby who has just been born.

D: This is an ordinary night, but God can do extra-ordinary things at any time.

This night a miracle happened.

In the Christmas story we encounter the poor and the rich, the cultured and the unwashed, those who give orders and those who carry them out, the good and the bad. The Christmas story is a wonder-filled story.

I am an angel. I am a messenger from God. The message is…

All: God is with us.

C: Even donkeys, hee-haw!

A Christmas Story

To make puppets

- Draw characters on A4 paper then glue or staple to similar sized pieces of cardboard, or
- Starting with the cardboard, stick on large Christmas stickers; figures cut from a nativity story book; nativity flannel-graph pictures, or
- Make collage faces – cut eyes from magazines, glue on wool hair, fabric head-gear etc.
- Attach each character-card to a stick or tube.
- Label the backs with the character's name and letter, or number.

Production notes

- Place the puppets face down on a long table in their A, B, C, groups before service/event begins.
- The four readers file in from stage left carrying their notes in their left hands and together sit behind the table.
- Each holds the appropriate puppet with their right hand when speaking. Hold the puppets on the right side, with bent elbows and hands at eye level. Hold the Angel high with arm straight.
- The words may be delivered in an 'over acted' style or deadpan flat.
- At the end all stand bow together and file off stage right with deadpan dignity leaving puppets and notes on the table. (For an extra laugh – Donkey reader picks up the Donkey puppet and as exiting steps aside for Angel then gives a last 'Hee-haw').

• • •

A Christmas Story (B)

A different script for each of the 9 individuals.

———————

A Christmas Story (B) 1 – Man

1 Man; 2 Woman; 3 Baby; 4 Inn-Keeper; 5 Bunch of Shepherds; 6 King; 7 Bunch of Wise-Guys; 8 Donkey; 9 Angel.

[Set 1] – **Man:** I am a man.

(After 'Angel') **All:** Together we make the Christmas Story.

[Set 2] – **Man:** I am a man. I am a tradesman.

(After 'Angel') **All:** Together we make the Christmas Story.

[Set 3] – **Man:** I am a man. I am a tradesman. I work hard.

(After 'Angel') **All:** Together we make the Christmas Story.

[Set 4] – **Man:** I am a man. I am a tradesman. I work hard. I am an –ordinary man.

(After 'Angel') **All:** Together we make the Christmas Story.

[Set 5] – **Man:** I am a man. I am a tradesman. I work hard. I am an – ordinary man. I am a peasant.

(After 'Angel') **All:** Together WE make the Christmas Story.

[Set 6] – **Man:** I am a man who has just become a father.

(After 'Angel') **All:** God is with us.

A Christmas Story (B) 2 – Woman

1 Man; **2 Woman**; 3 Baby; 4 Inn-Keeper; 5 Bunch of Shepherds; 6 King; 7 Bunch of Wise-Guys; 8 Donkey; 9 Angel.

[Set 1] – **Woman:** I am a woman.

(After 'Angel') **All:** Together we make the Christmas Story.

[Set 2] – **Woman:** I am a woman; not much more than a girl.

(After 'Angel') **All:** Together we make the Christmas Story.

[Set 3] – **Woman:** I am a woman; not much more than a girl. I have travelled a long way.

(After 'Angel') **All:** Together we make the Christmas Story.

[Set 4] – **Woman:** I am a woman; not much more than a girl. I have travelled a long way, and I have become a mother.

(After 'Angel') **All:** Together we make the Christmas Story.

[Set 5] – **Woman:** I am a woman; not much more than a girl. I have travelled a long way, and I have become a mother –a very new mother.

(After 'Angel') **All:** Together WE make the Christmas Story.

[Set 6] – **Woman:** I am a woman who has just given birth.

(After 'Angel') **All:** God is with us.

A Christmas Story (B) 3 – Baby

1 Man; 2 Woman; **3 Baby**; 4 Inn-Keeper; 5 Bunch of Shepherds; 6 King; 7 Bunch of Wise-Guys; 8 Donkey; 9 Angel.

[Set 1] – **Baby:** I am a baby.

(After 'Angel') **All:** Together we make the Christmas Story.

[Set 2] – **Baby:** I am a baby. I've just been born.

(After 'Angel') **All:** Together we make the Christmas Story.

[Set 3] – **Baby:** I am a baby. I've just been born – this is a new beginning.

(After 'Angel') **All:** Together we make the Christmas Story.

[Set 4] – **Baby:** I am a baby. I've just been born – this is a new beginning. I am a new baby.

(After 'Angel') **All:** Together we make the Christmas Story.

[Set 5] – **Baby:** I am a baby. I've just been born – this is a new beginning. I am a new baby. I am a special baby.

(After 'Angel') **All:** Together WE make the Christmas Story.

[Set 6] – **Baby:** I am a baby.

(After 'Angel') **All:** God is with us.

A Christmas Story (B) 4 – Inn-Keeper

1 Man; 2 Woman; 3 Baby; **4 Inn-Keeper**; 5 Bunch of Shepherds;
6 King; 7 Bunch of Wise-Guys; 8 Donkey; 9 Angel.

[Set 1] – **Inn-Keeper:** I am an inn-keeper.

(After 'Angel') **All:** Together we make the Christmas Story.

[Set 2] – **Inn-Keeper:** I am an inn-keeper. My inn is overflowing.

(After 'Angel') **All:** Together we make the Christmas Story.

[Set 3] – **Inn-Keeper:** I am an inn-keeper. My inn is overflowing. Travellers are sleeping in my stable.

(After 'Angel') **All:** Together we make the Christmas Story.

[Set 4] – **Inn-Keeper:** I am an inn-keeper. My inn is overflowing. Travellers are sleeping in my stable. I couldn't turn them away.

(After 'Angel') **All:** Together we make the Christmas Story.

[Set 5] – **Inn-Keeper:** I am an inn-keeper. My inn is overflowing. Travellers are sleeping in my stable. I couldn't turn them away. This is a new thing for me.

(After 'Angel') **All:** Together WE make the Christmas Story.

[Set 6] – (After 'Angel') **All:** God is with us.

A Christmas Story (B) 5 – Bunch of Shepherds

1 Man; 2 Woman; 3 Baby; 4 Inn-Keeper; **5 Bunch of Shepherds**; 6 King; 7 Bunch of Wise-Guys; 8 Donkey; 9 Angel.

[Set 1] – **Shepherds**: I am a bunch of shepherds.

(After 'Angel') **All:** Together we make the Christmas Story.

[Set 2] – **Shepherds:** We shepherds have to watch sheep at night.

(After 'Angel') **All:** Together we make the Christmas Story.

[Set 3] – **Shepherds:** We shepherds have to watch sheep at night. We are poor and smelly.

(After 'Angel') **All:** Together we make the Christmas Story.

[Set 4] – **Shepherds:** We shepherds have to watch sheep at night. We are poor and smelly. We are marginalised people.

(After 'Angel') **All:** Together we make the Christmas Story.

[Set 5] – **Shepherds:** We shepherds have to watch sheep at night. We are poor and smelly. We are marginalised people but this night we saw something special. So special we left our sheep and went on a journey.

(After 'Angel') **All:** Together WE make the Christmas Story.

[Set 6] – (After 'Angel') **All:** God is with us.

A Christmas Story (B) 6 – King

1 Man; 2 Woman; 3 Baby; 4 Inn-Keeper; 5 Bunch of Shepherds;
6 King; 7 Bunch of Wise-Guys; 8 Donkey; 9 Angel.

[Set 1] – **King:** I am a king.

(After 'Angel') **All:** Together we make the Christmas Story.

[Set 2] – **King:** I am a king. I give orders.

(After 'Angel') **All:** Together we make the Christmas Story.

[Set 3] – **King:** I am a king. I give orders. I am powerful and rich.

(After 'Angel') **All:** Together we make the Christmas Story.

[Set 4] – **King:** I am a king. I give orders. I am powerful and rich. My journey is to be great.

(After 'Angel') **All:** Together we make the Christmas Story.

[Set 5] – **King:** I am a king. I give orders. I am powerful and rich. My journey is to be great. I don't care who I hurt in the process.

(After 'Angel') **All:** Together WE make the Christmas Story.

[Set 6] – (After 'Angel') **All:** God is with us.

A Christmas Story (B) 7 – Bunch of Wise-Guys

1 Man; 2 Woman; 3 Baby; 4 Inn-Keeper; 5 Bunch of Shepherds;
6 King; **7 Bunch of Wise-Guys**; 8 Donkey; 9 Angel.

[Set 1] – **Wise-guys:** I am a bunch of wise-guys.

(After 'Angel') **All:** Together we make the Christmas Story.

[Set 2] – **Wise-guys:** We wise-guys are educated and cultured.

(After 'Angel') **All:** Together we make the Christmas Story.

[Set 3] – **Wise-guys:** We wise-guys are educated; cultured and clean.

(After 'Angel') **All:** Together we make the Christmas Story.

[Set 4] – **Wise-guys:** We wise-guys are educated; cultured and clean; despite having travelled from afar.

(After 'Angel') **All:** Together we make the Christmas Story.

[Set 5] – **Wise-guys:** We wise-guys are educated and cultured; and clean; despite having travelled from afar. We bring spices and gold.

(After 'Angel') **All:** Together WE make the Christmas Story.

[Set 6] – (After 'Angel') **All:** God is with us.

A Christmas Story (B) 8 – Donkey

1 Man; 2 Woman; 3 Baby; 4 Inn-Keeper; 5 Bunch of Shepherds; 6 King; 7 Bunch of Wise-Guys; **8 Donkey**; 9 Angel.

[Set 1] – **Donkey:** I am a donkey.

(After 'Angel') **All:** Together we make the Christmas Story.

[Set 2] – **Donkey:** I am a donkey. Hee-haw.

(After 'Angel') **All:** Together we make the Christmas Story.

[Set 3] – **Donkey:** I am a donkey. Hee-haw. Hee-haw.

(After 'Angel') **All:** Together we make the Christmas Story.

[Set 4] – **Donkey:** I am a donkey. Hee-haw. Hee-haw. Hee-haw.

(After 'Angel') **All:** Together we make the Christmas Story.

[Set 5] – **Donkey:** I am a donkey. Hee-haw. Hee-haw.

(After 'Angel') **All:** Together WE make the Christmas Story.

[Set 6] – (After 'Angel') **All:** God is with us.

Donkey: Even Donkeys… hee-haw!

A Christmas Story (B) 9 – Angel

1 Man; 2 Woman; 3 Baby; 4 Inn-Keeper; 5 Bunch of Shepherds; 6 King; 7 Bunch of Wise-Guys; 8 Donkey; **9 Angel.**

[Set 1] – **Angel:** I am an angel.

All: Together we make the Christmas Story.

[Set 2] – **Angel:** I am an angel. I am a messenger from God.

All: Together we make the Christmas Story.

[Set 3] – **Angel:** I am an angel. I am a messenger from God. The message is amazing.

All: Together we make the Christmas Story.

[Set 4] – **Angel:** I am an angel; a messenger from God. The message is amazing. The story is wonderful.

All: Together we make the Christmas Story.

[Set 5] – **Angel:** I am an angel; a messenger from God. The message is amazing. The story is wonderful. It's Awesome!

All: Together we make the Christmas Story.

[Set 6] – **Man:** I am a man who has just become a father.

Woman: I am a woman who has just become a mother.

Baby: I am a baby who has just been born

Angel: This is an ordinary night, but God can do extra-ordinary things at any time. This night a miracle happened. In the Christmas Story we encounter the poor and the rich, the cultured and the unwashed, those who give orders and those who carry them out, the good and the bad. The Christmas story is a wonder-filled story.
I am an angel. I am a messenger from God. The message is…

All: God is with us.

Story Telling in Church

Children's stories read in church are often aided by projected PowerPoint images, particularly during Advent.

Nativity stories are ideal for "audience" participation. Some scholars suggest that Luke's presentation of the birth stories were written in pageant form.

To involve a congregation through audience participation requires little preparation other than a brief practise of responses before reading (or telling) a story and perhaps some cue-cards for an assistant to hold up at the appropriate times.

Most Christmas stories mention animals (even though the Bible only names sheep). Picture books often tell the story from the point of view of a child or an animal. Every time an animal is mentioned the audience can give the traditional 'story noise' for that animal. (To avoid possible chaos, restrict each sound to two repeats), e.g. hee-haw-hee-haw; baa-baa; woof-woof; meow-meow, moo-moo, squeak-squeak, coo-coo, etc.

Some stories lend themselves to refrains being added such as a spoken phrase or a clap. If the central character is a child, it may be suitable to add a descriptive refrain such as:

- *Cue:* The shepherd boy was always… *(refrain)* **looking for adventures…**
- *Cue:* That night the inn keeper's daughter… *(refrain)* **couldn't get to sleep…**
- Everyone can shout the unforgettable words of the inn-keeper: **"No room!"**

Other alternatives may include the narrator (in the pulpit) assisted by one or more persons who say the spoken words (from the lectern).

And/or children dressed for the part walking on and saying brief memorised words to a hand-held wireless microphone.

Ten Plays +

Below are the cues and refrains I used when reading the story Jesus Christmas Party by Nicholas Allan

- *Cue:* there was a knock … at the door – *Response:* ***(Clap-clap)***
- *Cue:* the grumpy inn keeper shut … the door – *Response:* **(CLAP)**
- *Cue:* The inn keeper shouted … – *Response:* **"ROUND THE BACK"**

After reading a Christmas story it works well to have it followed by a cheerful carol such as Hark the Herald Angels Sing or Carol our Christmas our Upside-down Christmas. Invite the children to dance as they sing either up the front particularly if costumed (symbolic sheep ears, crowns, wings and haloes) or just jive with their parents in their pews.

· · ·

About these Plays

Lay preacher Rosalie Sugrue's short plays and meditations are ideal to present in church. They encourage us to engage with Bible and historical characters and explore important themes. Staging is simple. Few props or costumes are required.

Unless marked [adults] these play readings are suitable for children to present. Most work best with a combination of children and adults.

Summary of the Plays

Mary Jones' Walk — for a family service or Bible Sunday in July. Relive the story of the 15-year-old Welsh girl who walked 25 miles in search of a Bible and by doing so helped inspire the founding of Bible Society.

When The Treaty came to Mangungu — for a Waitangi Day celebration in early February. An historic event told from the perspective of Rev John Hobbs' 11-year-old daughter Emma.

Easter Women [adults] — for Lent, March/April. Listen in on five women who may have shared a room on that Saturday night so long ago: Mary of Nazareth – the mother of Jesus, Mary Magdalene alias Mary of Bethany, the 'other' Mary, Joanna and Salome.

About these Plays

ANZAC Day — for the Sunday closest to 25 April. Two children learn more about their family connection with World War One. Suitable for presenting in church when reflecting on war.

The Wesley Saga — for any Wesley Celebration or Wesley Day, May. A rhyming romp through the family history of Samuel and Susanna Wesley, sons John and Charles and their sisters.

How Lay Preaching Began — John Wesley, still an Anglican clergyman, is upset that Thomas Maxwell, a layperson, has preached at The Foundery without John's permission. Susanna helps John to see lay people preaching as an opportunity rather than a problem. (Ideal for Lay Preachers' Sunday, 2nd Sunday in August.)

Go and Tell — The Woman of Samaria meets other village women at the well and explains how her meeting with Jesus has changed her life. She also regains the friendship of these women who had previously shunned her.

A Peace Presentation [adults] — any time, or Peace Sunday, early August. Monologues of two women from the scrolls of Hebrew Scriptures and two from the pages of New Zealand history. Ordinary women who by wit and will were each peace achievers.

Mahlah & Sisters — a justice issue Bible story for any time of year. Five capable daughters successfully lobby for women to be able to own land.

Mahlah & Sisters (B); The Daughters of Zelophehad — the same story told in less words, suitable for devotions at fellowships, house groups and youth groups.

Christmas Women [adults] — multiple uses during Advent. Five meditations of women sharing their encounters with Mary for use in advent worship: Elizabeth (Mary's cousin) talks with Anna; Anne (Mary's mother); Woman Traveller; Inn-keeper's Wife; Anna (the prophetess).

No Room — for Advent, Christmas & Christian World Service celebrations. Makes a thought-provoking link between refugees arriving by boat at Christmas Island and Mary & Joseph finding no room at the inn.

Ten Plays +

A Christmas Story — for Advent and Christmas. 13 stick puppets. Theme: God is with us.

A Christmas Story (B) — a second version of *A Christmas Story* with 9 separate pages of 9 separate scripts for 9 people.

Story Telling in Church — gives readers suggestions for easy and simple ways to add drama to Bible stories in church.

• • •

About the Author

Rosalie May Sugrue is a wife, mother and grandmother. She is a retired teacher and motellier with a background in Bible study.

Rosalie is a past National Programme Convenor of the NZ Methodist Women's Fellowship; a past Vice President of NZMWF, is a past Wellington District Convenor of MWF and currently co-facilitator of Kapiti's Afternoon Women's Fellowship; an active lay preacher, a past President of the NZ Lay Preachers Association; the inaugural Facilitator of the NZ Methodist Lay Preachers Network, a past member of the Churches Agency on Social Issues; and a past member of the Community of Women and Men in Church and Society.

Retired to the Kapiti Coast Rosalie has been active in MWF, National Council of Women, Victim Support and U3A. She has plays, poems, prayers, Bible puzzles and articles published in many church magazines in NZ including a regular Bible Challenge puzzle in Touchstone. She also has work included in devotional anthologies in Canada, the UK and the US. Her prayers have been used in diverse national conferences including Baptist Women in America and Bishops in Ireland.

Also by Rosalie Sugrue
from Philip Garside Publishing Ltd

Sophia and Daughters Revisited: *Reflections on Women of Biblical Connection* **(2019)**: Rediscover these characters as spirited, wise women of passion and compassion. Now includes Tamar, Dinah, Naomi, Michal, Vashti, Jephthah's Daughter, Lenna Button, Susanna Wesley and Ann Turner to use in church during the sermon slot.

Lay Preaching Basics: *A Practical Guide to Leading Worship* **(2018)**: Do you want to learn how to preach and lead worship, but don't know where to start? This practical guide by experienced Methodist Lay Preacher Rosalie Sugrue will get you going.

Theme Scheme: *Creative Ideas, Activities, Games, Puzzles, Plays, Quizzes* **(Updated 2018)**: Offers you a wealth of creative ideas, activities, games, puzzles and quizzes to help plan, organise and lead your group's programmes. All are fun and practical, requiring minimal equipment, and time to prepare. (In Print & eBooks)

The League of Lilith: *A thriller with soul. Written with her son Troy Sugrue* **(2013)**: Sarai, a Biblical Studies lecturer, learns a terrible truth; a core knowledge she must impart to a successor. Will she choose society wife, Jen, or bondage and discipline prostitute Kat? An explosive novel with a dramatic climax. (eBooks)

Ten Plays +

Greens and Greys (2015): Journey with Molly Sinclair through her 1950s childhood on the West Coast, her move to Christchurch for teacher training, drama-filled OE in the UK and Europe, and as she returns to NZ in the mid-1960s. An engaging coming-of-age tale. (In Print & eBooks)

Green, Ho! (2015):
Green, Ho! is an extended version of *Greens and Greys* that adds another dimension in the form of hidden disability. (In Print & eBooks)

Free PDF eBook edition offer

To help you stage these plays, the publisher is happy to provide a free PDF eBook edition of *Ten Plays* to anyone who has purchased a print copy.

The PDF will be password protected. You will be provided with the password which you will need to enter each time you open the PDF file.

You can then copy and paste the text of the play into a word processing file or print off pages direct from the PDF.

To get your free PDF, please email books@pgpl.co.nz and tell us where you bought your print copy.

www.ingramcontent.com/pod-product-compliance
Lightning Source LLC
Chambersburg PA
CBHW071500070526
44578CB00001B/397